# THE RELUCTANT MOUNTAIN GOAT

L**OUISE** F**ERRARO** D**ERETCHIN**

*Louise Deretchin*

S**TARSHINE** P**RESS**

*Spring, Texas*

*A memoir of my journey from galas in Texas to plywood-walled inns in the Himalayas*

*August 31-September 17, 2011*

*To my husband Joel who has made our lives together an adventure.*

# CONTENTS

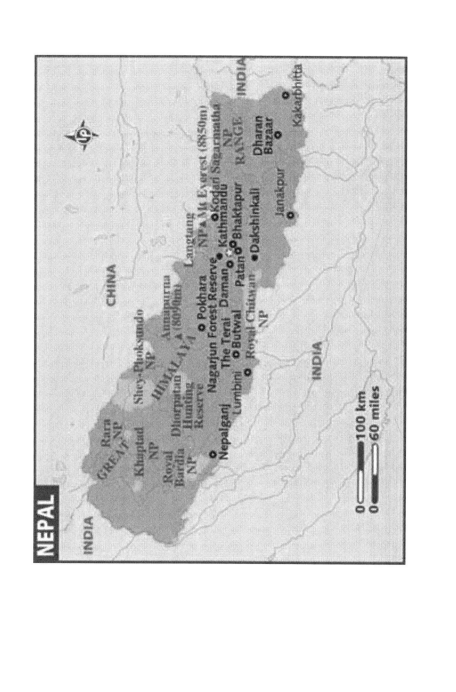

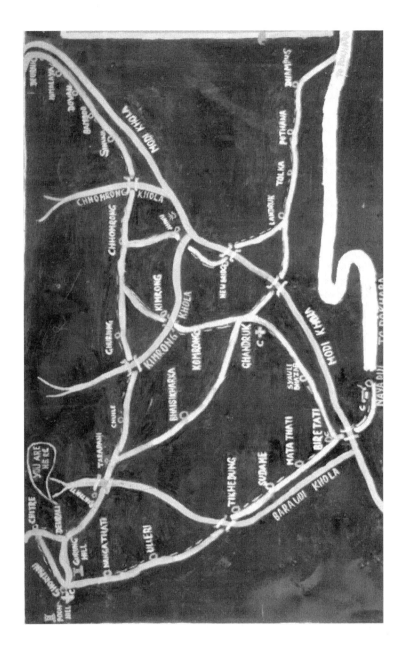

ANNAPURNA TREKKING TRAILS

## Chapter One

# TRIPPED

I'm done with the ritual of coating my face with color. I blot my lipstick, smooth the front of my basic-black evening gown and check my rhinestone earrings in the mirror. I've taken my time, dragged my feet, but I can't delay any longer.

"C'mon. Forget the damn bracelet. We're already late," my pacing husband calls to me as I head down the stairs and remember the matching bracelet I had planned to wear. With his peppered gray hair cut short, and slim athletic body he looks absolutely scrumptious even though his lined face reveals a no-nonsense seriousness.

I dread going to large social events where smiles are the most important accessory and conversation is kept light enough to float across the room without landing on anyone's pet peeve. I'm strictly a small-group person; my husband, on the other hand, could live in a glass house with "Welcome" plastered all over it.

When the invitation to the gala arrived last month, he had asked if we could put it on our calendar. Of course I said yes. How could I say no when he was sweet enough to ask? Besides, after being coaxed out of the house the evening of a big bash, I usually surprise myself by having a good time.

The cocktail hour is half over by the time we arrive. Clusters of partyers in glittering gowns and sleek tuxedoes crowd the lobby and saturate the air with laughter-filled conversation.

Side-by-side silent auction items clutter cloth-covered tables. A train of guests divides its time between chatting and writing down bids as it inches along the tables. I fortify myself against the temptation of joining the line. Joel and I are still reeling from the expense of moving into a new home we bought at auction three months ago. It was my hand that flew up into the air to win the bid and then shook violently as I placed my signature next to Joel's on the contract that committed us to a new home.

As I struggle with myself, repeating the pledge Joel and I made not to bid on anything, a nameless face approaches with his hand extended toward my husband.

"Joel! So glad you could be here. Louise! I haven't seen you in a long time."

"Joel keeps me hidden." That's not true. I just happen to like doing solitary things—writing and painting or taking unscheduled walks.

Most people don't know who I am unless I appear by Joel's side. He steps away and I stand uninterrupted, entertaining my own thoughts until he returns. From my vantage point of stillness I can spot the volunteers who have worked hard to plan this event. Their broad smiles and searching eyes radiate pride and purpose as they slip between guests to make sure everything runs smoothly. One of the volunteers in a shimmering silver gown approaches me after Joel joins the queue at the bar. She looks familiar; but I can't place who she is.

"Hey, Louise! You look great. I just saw Joel. He said you don't have a bid package. I'll get one for you."

"Oh, no. Don't bother. We'll take care of it."

"Don't be silly. It's no trouble at all. I'll be right back."

I don't want a bid package. But five minutes later, there I stand with temptation in my hand.


A chime signals it's time to enter the banquet room. Crystal chandeliers, soft lighting, floral centerpieces, tables set with china, silver, and wine glasses make the whole room sparkle. Proud of our self-control at bypassing the silent auction, my husband and I high-five each other and enter.

"Did you bid on anything?" friends ask before we can make it to our table.

"We tried not to," is our noncommittal reply.

We work our way past numbered tables and finally arrive at ours. It's right up front, much too close to where the action will take place. We won't be able to duck out unnoticed before the live auction begins.

We shake hands with the people at our table and take our seats. The din of conversation wanes as the master of ceremonies approaches the podium. We peruse the brochure of live auction items while short speeches are made and we wait for dinner to be served.

A forty-four carat oval-cut citrine, a wine collection, a gourmet barbecue dinner at someone's house—no problem, these are things I know we can pass up. It'll be easy to sit on our hands. I read on. Then I see it. It's on the last page:

Package Six: *Eat, Pray, Love in Gokarna Forest Resort*
*in Exotic Kathmandu, Nepal*
*Includes airfare for two with the two-week stay*

Anxiety trickles through my body. I can't count the number of times Joel has said he wants to trek in the Himalayas and has tried to convince me it would be fun. Each time I greet his testing-the-waters with a noncommittal smile while *you-can-go-just-leave-me-out-of-it* pulsates behind my eyes. Walking on rocks for hours and falling into a crevice never to resurface hold no appeal for me.

I slip a quick sideways glance toward Joel and see he has reached the last page of the auction items list. I turn away and fix my eyes on a waiter, a chandelier, a door—anything but the brochure or Joel.

He turns to me; his expressionless face barely masks the hope that lies behind it. In a soft, even voice he says, "Did you see Package Six?"

Of course I've seen it! The words *forest* and *exotic* in the description of the package have been playing Ping-Pong in my brain for the last five minutes. They keep bouncing off my retina flashing images of a tree house with a vine used to descend to a communal commode. But when I look at his pleading puppy eyes, I can't bring myself to give a flat-out "No".

"I saw it." Big pause . . . "Would you like to bid on it?" Foolish even to ask.

"Yes."

Trapped!

"What are you willing to bid?" he asks. Most trips at charitable galas we have attended sold for $15,000 to $20,000 and sometimes more.

"Eight thousand," I offer—high enough to give Joel hope, low enough to let me feel safe we would not win the bid.

Dinner is done. Lights go up. The auction begins. After what seems like no more than a few minutes, the bidding opens for Package Six. The wine served at dinner must have put bidders in a generous mood. The final bids on Packages One through Five were high. I relax.

Joel's calm concentration does little to hide the eagerness behind it. Two bidders are bidding against each other for the Nepal trip.

"One thousand."

"Fifteen hundred."

"Seventeen hundred."

Their hands jut up one right after the other.

"Two thousand."

I start to sweat—the increments are too small.

"Twenty-five hundred."

"I have twenty-five hundred. Now let me have $3,000."

Silence.

Oh no! This is crazy. Don't they know airfare alone is about $4,000?

"Three thousand, three thousand, let me have $3,000. What about $2,700?" The auctioneer tries to tease a higher bid out of the second bidder. No dice. The auctioneer scans the room, "Twenty-seven hundred. Anyone?" No takers.

With gavel raised, in rapid succession he declares, "Going once. Going twice . . ."

I hold my breath waiting to hear "Sold" before Joel has time to react; but Joel's right arm, holding the paddle with our bid number, springs up faster than the gavel comes down. We enter the bidding war at $2,700.

"I have $2,700, now give me $3,000."

The remaining bidder ups the price; but in the rapid-fire bidding battle that ensues, he must sense the determination that has taken control of Joel's bidding arm. At $4,000 the other bidder quits. This time the gavel drops and the "Sold" means Package Six is ours. My heart sinks.

Early Sunday morning, I sit at my desk at home checking email; a band of sunlight slices across the room. I can't bring myself to look up Gokarna Forest Resort on the Internet. I'm in denial and want to stay there. Joel, on the other hand, wants to see what last night's prize looks like.

Seated at his desk set against the wall, his back is turned toward me and his eyes are aimed at his computer screen. "Louise, you have to see this," he says with a voice that betrays his restrained excitement.

"I'm not interested. I want to be surprised."

"Gokarna Forest Resort is a FIVE-STAR resort!"

What? No planks in a treetop? I peek over his shoulder and see that the list of amenities includes a swimming pool and a spa. Okay, I can handle this—luxury and pampering for two weeks. Better yet, the resort is located far away from the Himalayas.

As it turns out, not quite far enough.

## Chapter Two

# IS IT STILL TODAY?

*Wednesday, August 31*

Sandra's words linger in my mind as I enter through the middle door of the airplane, "Coach on Qatar Airways is like first class." She has been to Nepal several times and helped me make my trip arrangements.

I have never had the privilege of turning left into first class, so I automatically turn right where our seats will be. We enter a cabin that has seats arranged two abreast with plenty of leg room and side-to-side space. This looks promising.

I pass numbered rows none of which has my seat number on it. Hope dims as I see yet another opening into a darker chamber where the aircraft appears to narrow. I step through the opening and see nine seats across in groups of three. The hips of passengers walking ahead of me bump the seats on either side of the ribbon-wide aisle.

Joel shows no disappointment; he did not have raised expectations. Besides, he sits on the aisle while I get to sit in the middle between him and a stranger, my prize for being built small.

Unlike the thin, cardboard seats we've traveled on in the past that have as much room for passengers as egg cartons have for eggs, these seats are comfortably padded with a reasonable amount of elbow and leg room. I slip into my middle seat and nod to the portly, balding man who will be my right-side companion for the next many hours. We exchange pleasantries but not names. His accent tells me he is either British or Australian, I can't tell which. As I tuck my guidebooks into the pocket in front of me and arrange my pillow and blanket, I'm thankful the stranger next to me has not spilled over into my territory.

We have barely glanced at our tickets let alone read our travel guides. I reach for mine and see that Joel is fortifying himself with a nap for the work ahead. I tuck the guidebook back and put two stickers on the back of each of our seats. The symbol on one says, "Wake me up for food," the other, "Don't wake me up for duty-free shopping."

My watch says it's 2:00 A.M. Houston time. We've been on the plane four hours, passed at least one time zone, been movied, beveraged, and fed. An hour ago I lost the fight for an arm rest on my right side where the stranger sits. His abundant belly explains the need for the crescent-shaped indentation molded into the pull-down trays in front of us. His stomach squeezes into the contoured tray perfectly. He finishes an airplane-sized bottle of wine and orders another and another then settles back into semi-slumber.

I have my noise-reduction earphones on, but I'm not listening to anything, just trying to drown out the sounds leaking from the stranger's earphones and his slurred, mumbled, not-so-private sing-along. The unsolicited entertainment reaches its peak when the stranger belts out with gusto, "WE-ARE-THE-CHAMPIONS! WE-ARE-THE-CHAMPIONS!" After a few rounds of "Champions," he sings other songs, the lyrics of which I cannot and do not want to make out. I pray that he falls asleep and his elbow, which is now well over the armrest, doesn't encroach further into my shrinking space.

At last a light snore tells me he's sound asleep. I reach over and with several quick jabs at a button, lower the volume until no noise seeps from his earphones. Now I just wish a flight attendant would remove the coffee cup and other items the stranger set on my tray. In total oblivion, comfortable in his aisle seat, my husband sleeps. I take a deep sigh, think about reaching for a guidebook, but decide I'd better close my eyes for a while; it's the middle of the night.

I awake to the sound of metal beverage carts bumping down the aisles. Joel gives me a lazy look and asks, "Did you sleep well?"

"Uh-huh. And you?"

"I didn't sleep much," he replies.

That's not what I observed. He must count the twilight zone when he is half asleep as sleeping and not the unconscious state he slips into between twilights. I smile back knowingly, but do not contradict him, then reach for the travel guide in the seat pocket.

I read a few pages then double back on a sentence. Wait a minute! According to this guide September is still monsoon season. The guidebook I flipped through before the trip claimed monsoons occur May *to* NOT *through* September! I should have read *this* guide sooner. It says that rivers become dangerously swollen in September. Joel wants to go rafting. It would take witnessing a raft, complete with tourists and a guide, being swallowed by rapids to deter Joel, not just a sentence in a guidebook uncorroborated by a second guidebook.

My hands begin to sweat. I read on.

Trails turn into rivers of mud, roads become blocked by floods and landslides. Panic shoots through my brain. What are we doing here? Why are we going in the fall? Anti-leech oil? Flashlights?

I packed long skirts so I could *blend* with the Nepalis, as Sandra said I should. I'm glad I slipped two pairs of lightweight slacks in at the last minute—I may have to live in them for two weeks. I can't see walking around in sandals, dragged down by a soaking-wet skirt. I thought I was joking when I said I would send Joel into the wilderness and I would stay in the spa—I may have to do just that.

I put the guide aside and decide to let Joel figure out what we'll do for the next two weeks.


After fourteen hours of flying, we arrive in Doha, Qatar. My mind is as confused as my body over what time and day it is. A clock nearby tells me it's 7:30 pm, but not the day. I move the hands of my watch around giving up on Texas and body time. I'll find out the date when I arrive at Kathmandu. We have ahead of us a five-and-a-half hour layover in Doha, a three-and-a-half hour flight to Kathmandu, and I don't even want to know how long a drive to the resort.

I walk around the airport feeling like a dehydrated zombie. I'm torn between coffee and sleep, but choose the former afraid I'll miss my flight.

The Duty-Free shop is large enough to be the first floor of Bloomingdales; its prices are more like Tiffany's. Men with onyx eyes and skin the color of sun-roasted almonds move from aisle to aisle in long white robes, their heads covered with white or checkered red and white head dresses. They examine watches, cameras, and other electronics. Women and young girls covered head-to-toe in black-on-black embroidered abayas finger purses, try on jewelry, and sniff fragrances. Small children linger by toy displays. I try to take a picture of this elegant world, but a guard quickly lets me know it's not allowed.

I tuck my camera back in my purse and look down at my feet that are sending distress signals upward. Each one looks like a cross between a sausage and a pillow; one prick and they would explode. It's too late to put them up on something somewhere. It's time to board.

As we enter the narrow-bodied plane, it is clear that all luxury is gone. We're back to cardboard seats and shoulders compressed into allotted space. A woman occupies the window seat to my left; Joel has the aisle. She smiles tentatively at me; I don't feel up to conversation. Joel leans across me, makes introductions, and starts talking.

"Do you want to change seats?" runs through my mind. He could be as sociable as he cares to be if he sits in the middle. No such luck. He sits back and closes his eyes leaving me to continue what he started with as much of a smile as my exhausted self can muster.

The woman, Nanda Kulu, a native of Nepal, is dressed in dark slacks and a fitted, patterned blouse; her dark hair is tied back. She doesn't look the least bit tired even though she has traveled further than I have. She names places in Kathmandu, each three to four syllables long, and asks if we plan to visit them.

"We haven't made any plans yet," I reply.

"Come see me. I will tell you about Nepal, where to go, what to see."

Having a native guide our visit sounds a lot more interesting and easier than reading guidebooks.

"I have a travel agency. I'll take good care of you. Do you want to go to Poon Hill? You can see the high peaks from there."

I don't know what Poon Hill is, but it sounds interesting. As inconspicuously as one can in tight quarters, I nudge Joel and say, "Nanda has a travel agency. She is offering to set up an itinerary for us. Interested?"

"Go for it," he replies without hesitation. He must be as relieved as I am to have a plan, or at least the start of one.

"First come to my orphanage. I take care of thirty children there. Another fifty live at home—I help feed and send them to school. I was just in the United States to raise money."

Whoops! I guess we'll be making a donation.

"The children have prepared a show for tomorrow," Nanda continues. "Come see it. Then we'll go to my office and plan your visit."

I have to clarify what day *tomorrow* is. I don't know where I am in time, but I can get it straightened out at the resort if only I have the weekday name.

"Saturday," Nanda obliges me with an anchor point.

My mind is too groggy to grasp that I should not commit to anything that requires getting up early the next morning.

Chapter Three

# THE ARRIVAL

*Friday, September 2*

It's easy to spot our fellow long distance travelers as we exit the plane in Kathmandu. With worldly goods strapped to our backs, hung from our shoulders, and dragged behind us, we look more like refugees than tourists beginning their vacation. Sapped of energy, we blindly follow an invisible leader as we pass unsolicited offers of assistance.

"No thank you. We can take care of our luggage," I say with a smile, eyes fixed straight ahead, feet set on automatic, refusing to interrupt the steady trudge forward. Joel and I drag one large bag and one carry-on each. Joel has an added backpack, the weight of which would turn me into an upended turtle.

Doggedly, I follow the crowd through the grayness of the barebones airport; my eyes are set on the exit. Before I can muster a "Don't" someone snatches our bags and loads them onto a conveyor belt at what I hope is the last X-ray point. The clothes in my suitcase have been screened so many times they must be radioactive by now. We walk to the left of the machine. By the time we reach the other side, we find a different man loading our luggage onto a cart.

I am about to stop the man when Joel says, "It's okay. Let him do his job." Baggage loaded, Joel peels a couple of singles from a small pile of bills and gives them to the cart loader.

A few feet away someone holds a card with our last name on it. He takes hold of the cart and pushes it no more than fifty feet to a car with a driver standing at its side, loads our luggage into the trunk, and makes it clear he wants a tip. Joel peels off another two singles.

"One more," says the cart-pusher.

Joel looks blank; his brain cells must be dozing.

I nudge him, "He wants another dollar."

"No. One more," says the man then points to the money at the bottom of the pile in Joel's hand and makes it clear he wants a bill with a two-digit number not one.

"I'm-not-giving-you-ten-dollars!" Each word out of Joel's mouth drips with indignation. The two-dollar tip must start looking good to the cart-pusher because, with a nod and a smile, he takes it. I'm surprised Joel lets him have it.


It must have rained into the car. A towel covers the backseat, but the dampness seeps through. I forget about the moisture as the driver zigzags through unnamed streets on our way to the resort. I count my blessings we didn't rent a car and attempt the drive on our own. Our vacation would have begun with an argument as Joel negotiated potholes and pedestrians through unfamiliar streets, requested, and then demanded directions I would have been helpless to provide.

Plus driving is on the left-side of the road except for passing which is done by heading directly into oncoming traffic. Inches separate each moving object—human or otherwise. My guidebook claims the best way to get around Kathmandu is by bike. The author must be waging a vendetta against tourists—riding a bike appears suicidal.

Traffic in Kathmandu as seen from the backseat of the car.

My nose rejects the fumes spewing from the wall of vehicles in front of us, but my lungs say, "Do it!" I break down and inhale as shallowly as I can, but fear I will need a lung transplant after two-weeks in Kathmandu. Then I realize I may not have to worry about that at all if I don't survive the traffic.


Slim figures of women, some dressed in tunics over slacks, others in saris in shades of gold, orange, and red, float along smog-shrouded roads. The women move alongside trucks, buses, cars, and motorbikes without flinching. Forms flicker in and out of the smog converting the scene into a surrealist painting come to life.

Open-air shops the width of a double garage line both sides of the streets. Shopkeepers casually watch over their pots and pans, plastic buckets, food, or clothing hung on walls or stacked in piles. Small mountains of dirt lay heaped along either side of the street. A man stands on a pile of red stones. He swings a hammer and sends it crashing down. While the blows come one after another, the pile appears unchanged. I think of a question a college professor once asked: "How long would it take to wear down a mountaintop if a bird's wing brushes against it each time it circles the mountain?"

I'm usually chatty, excited about what I see when we journey to new places. But this time Joel and I travel in silence; the silence says plenty.

We pass a man with a basket that covers his back from the top of his shoulders to his thighs. Another worker shovels stones into the basket. The stones will be transported on the back of the laborer to a construction site.

Cows graze along the side of the road and amble into the street, adding to the traffic confusion. They are sacred, cared for, milked, but not eaten.

"If a cow falls and dies *maybe* someone will eat it," the driver tells us.

I think of institutions back home that earn the title "sacred cows." But, unlike cows, they seem immune to death from natural causes. I take a picture of a cow from my car window, but I'm too close and get only its rump.

At the outskirts of town we reach flat, open spaces. Two and three story buildings that are hollow concrete shells dot the landscape. The area looks as if it exists at the intersection of construction and destruction. Its buildings are either being built or torn down; I can't tell which. At a bend in the road, I see a large field of garbage on either side. I find out later that Kathmandu is experiencing a building boom, but that the city hasn't planned for services such as garbage collection to accommodate the growth.

It's at the garbage field that whatever remains of my image of meandering through cobblestone streets, discovering quaint shops and restaurants shrivels then disappears. It leaves me wondering what I will do for two weeks. I settle back into silence; it's time to let my mind go blank.

Forty-five minutes after leaving the airport, we make a left turn through a guarded gate and continue up a curving road into the Gokarna Forest Resort. My expectations are not high; I have left room for surprise or disappointment.

The road, free of potholes, winds past trees that are at least twelve feet wide and over seventy feet tall. They are set against a backdrop of densely-packed rain forest.

"Those trees are enormous. What are they?" I ask.

"Those are rubber trees. They are two hundred years old. All of Kathmandu used to be like this."

We pull up to the front of a two-story, brick building with a tile-shingled roof and a pagoda entry. A man stands ready to greet us at the glass doors that open into the lobby. He has on a thigh-length white cotton shirt topped with a gray vest, baggy white trousers that taper in at the ankle, and a cylindrical hat the same color as his vest.

His hands pressed together at his chest, fingers pointed upward, he bows his head slightly and says with a smile, "Namaste."

As I return the greeting I start to feel hope resurging.

The Gokarna Forest Resort main building.

Greeting at the entrance. "Namaste."

Beyond the glass doors a wide marble entry with wicker chairs and ancient sculptures runs left and right. A spotless glass wall opposite where I stand overlooks a grassy area lined with shops to the right and art-filled corridors to the left. The natural light and flow of fresh air render the lobby serene but not static. I try to act cool and sophisticated, but all I want to say is "Wow!"

My eyes barely finish surveying the lobby when the hostess says, "Your room won't be ready for a while. You must be tired. We will give you a temporary room to rest in until yours is available."

The room dwarfs ones I've stayed in at Hyatts and Fairmonts. A black wood and wicker headboard for the king-size platform bed rests against a floor-to-ceiling brick wall. Tightly woven macramé chairs sit across the room next to a glass-top table. A cream-colored sculptured sofa made from resin lines part of another wall. In a separate room are an American-style commode, a pedestal sink, and a five-foot square grey cement shower.

"Will our room be like this?" I ask.

"The same."

I think we have struck gold.


Hunger wakes me from a two-hour nap. I nudge Joel. "C'mon. Let's get something to eat."

He answers, "Okay," but doesn't move. It takes more aggressive shaking and a tantalizing description of food to wake him from his stupor and get him out of bed.

It's 4:30 in the afternoon—monkey time, the time of day when slim-bodied, gold-colored monkeys come out to play. They climb along building ledges, walls, and windows. Some carry babies hanging under their bellies and move with such agility it's hard to believe a baby is in tow. I grab the closest camera, Joel's, open the window and slide back the screen to get a better picture. His camera lens is too big; I decide to run for mine which lies next to some pretzels on a table clear across the room.

"I hope they don't come in," I call to Joel as I bolt across the floor.

"Too late, there in."

Three monkeys shoot past me, grab the bag of pretzels, and head back toward the window to a chorus of "Out! Out! Out!" from me and random noises accompanied by herding arm swings from Joel. The last one to exit becomes tangled in the drapes and receives a gentle assist from Joel. I slide the window closed, breathe a sigh of relief, and then realize I didn't get a picture.

We leave our unpacked bags ready for the staff to move to our room for the two-week stay.

Along the stone path to the clubhouse restaurant we pass the spa, a separate building nestled in trees. On the opposite side of the path, set back in the forest, three monkeys lounge in a pagoda-shaped gazebo. It looks as if the gazebo were built for their pleasure instead of ours.

We head down broad flights of stairs to the restaurant and choose a table overlooking the golf course.

A breeze blows in from the open glass doors. The sun is low in the sky, golfers are finishing their rounds, and deer graze on the hilly, forest-rimmed course. Views of mountains topped with blue sky and billowing clouds rise beyond. I am almost ready to forget the twenty-nine hours of traveling and the drive from the airport.

Joel, relaxed, points to monkeys sitting on the golf course green. "I think they are watching the sunset with us."

Eager to get started on our adventure, he begins to talk about tours and hikes. I want to spend a day lounging by the indoor pool, exploring the grounds, watching monkeys play in the rubber trees, and getting a couple's massage at the spa. I visualize tying down Joel for twenty-four hours to do this. But tomorrow, Saturday, I'll have to slacken the rope; we promised to visit Nanda Kulu's orphanage and her travel agency. Meanwhile, this evening, I will enjoy gardens, cool breezes, and the platform bed.

Chapter Four

# UP AND OUT

*Saturday, September 3*

"Blend! Wear long skirts." Sandra's words had sent me last-minute shopping for ankle-length skirts. My Texas friend has been to Nepal several times. Now here I stand in my white, multi-tiered skirt that makes me look ten pounds heavier than I am. Its black sister hangs in the closet of our room. I make note to avoid mirrors for the next two weeks.

I wonder why we agreed to have a driver pick us up at 9:00 a.m. to go to Nanda's orphanage. By noon I'll feel like a deflated balloon; but right now I feel surprisingly good. Perhaps jet lag has whooshed by like the hands of the clock that sped through the eleven time zones we crossed to get here.

As Joel and I stroll into the lobby ten minutes late we see that the driver has made himself at home chatting with the resort staff. I take a breath and brace for the ride through Kathmandu. The orphanage, it turns out, is on the far side of the city—I get extra white-knuckle time.

The address written on a piece of paper is of no use to the driver who is unfamiliar with the area in which the Mitrata-Nepal orphanage is located. He circles around the same blocks enough times to make them begin to look familiar before he gives up and borrows a phone from a shopkeeper to call Nanda. She is close by and comes to get us.

"Namaste. I am so glad you came to see my children." Her round face and broad smile radiate energy. A pink and white tunic worn over pleated, baggy pants tucked at the ankle replaces the western clothes she wore when we met her on the airplane yesterday. I revisit "blending in" and see that it is not going to happen. At five-foot three I stand half-a-head taller than Nanda. Her diminutive frame typical of Nepali women makes my 130 pounds feel like 200. Her tied-back hair—thick, dark, and long—lies in contrast to my mine—short, curly, and light. I envy the naturalness with which she wears a shear scarf draped across her neckline, its ends flowing down her back. Joel, with his slim physique, buttoned-up polo shirt, and khaki pants does a lot better job of blending even though his five-foot-nine height makes him tall among Nepalis.

We struggle to keep pace with what appears to be a leisurely stroll for Nanda. We whiz down sidewalks and across streets without breaking stride. I'm convinced by her masterful walk that an invisible signal passes between vehicles and pedestrians; each knows when he has lost his bid for a piece of the asphalt and yields to the other contender. Having grown up in Brooklyn I have a built-in signal of my own cultivated from years of crossing mid-block, weaving between trucks and cars. But my signal proves inadequate here. I walk with my toes a hair's breadth away from Nanda's heels trying to attach myself to whatever protects her from the onslaught of traffic, the pattern of which resembles a Jackson Pollock painting set in motion. Joel, who trails a few steps behind us, is on his own.

"Come, I have some people I want you to meet. They are my friends. You are my new friends," Nanda says as we enter the orphanage and climb three flights of gray concrete steps. Children's voices echo through the building carried on breezes that flow through open windows and doors. Brown-skin, barefoot boys and girls run up and down the steps, the youngest about five, the oldest fifteen, each careful to let us pass. Smiles, Namastes, and nods greet us.

"Fifty children live here. Some are at school today. Sorry they will miss you. The others are waiting to meet you. They have planned a special day."

On the third floor, Nanda slips off her shoes outside a door, we follow suit. Inside, the sunny room is filled with Americans. None of the women are wearing long skirts, just long slacks with short tops. The American friends serve on the orphanage's board and raise money for the orphanage. They "adopt" individual children for whom they provide funds for clothing, gifts, and private school education

"These are my new friends from Texas," Nanda explains to the group.

I hope they don't think oil wells, black gold, a new building!

We exchange names and talk about the orphanage as I try to ignore the humidity which converts my crisp cotton clothing to clinging cloth and my hair into tightly sprung ringlets. I didn't think it was possible to find a place on earth that could match, let alone surpass, the humidity back home in Houston. A teenage girl announces the music program is about to begin. Barefoot, we travel down the cool concrete steps to a second floor room where a patchwork of mats are spread on the floor facing the children already seated and poised to play. I head for a mat in the back corner of the room grateful my balloon-like skirt hides the gracelessness with which I begin to lower then plunk myself down.

The children, who look no older than twelve, bring their hands together, lower their eyes, and pray before they begin to play folk music on traditional Nepali instruments. A boy plays a sanrangi, a bowed, wooden stringed instrument, its sound squeaky by nature or by child—I don't know which. Another beats out a mellow sounding rhythm on a madal, a drum that tapers to each end and is held sideways so that both heads can be played at once. Three girls and a boy play melody on hand-carved flutes of light-colored, unfinished wood.

Concert at the Mitrata-Nepal orphanage.
Children playing Nepali flutes.

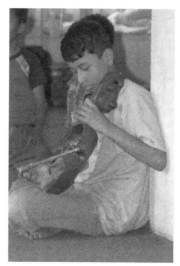

A child plays the Sarangi, a four-stringed traditional Nepali instrument.

I listen to the children play, but mostly watch their beautiful faces. I wish I could take at least half a dozen back home with me even though I am long-past the child rearing stage. It flashes through my mind that I could surprise my daughters with one or two additions to their families, but I suspect that wouldn't be appreciated. Besides, seeing the children's gentle joyfulness, I wouldn't want to remove any of them from their kindly Nepali culture to transplant them into the more aggressive American culture in which I live.

The concert ends and we move to the basement to see a dance performance. A girl combines traditional rhythms with contemporary hip juts and shoulder shrugs that I have seen my twelve-year-old granddaughter use. I want to take her home, too. The boldness of her dance changes to shyness after her dance is done and she heads back to her seat on the floor. A local volunteer takes the stage and moves his fiftyish, fleshy body through traditional Nepali dance movements and poses with surprising smoothness. Little boys mimic break dancers by spinning on their backs and contorting their bodies.

Girl at the orphanage dancing.

When the dance performance ends, the children rush to mingle with their guests. Their imperfect English seems perfect nonetheless. Their smiles make every pore in my body smile. They are beautiful inside and out, a characteristic I come to learn is inherent in the Nepali culture.

Nanda, standing by the stairs, says, "Come to the third floor. The children have prepared lunch for you."

As we are about to re-enter the sunny room we first entered, Joel glances at the pile of shoes outside the door and says, "My shoes are missing."

"Are you sure?" I scan the pile. His sneakers *are* gone. I give Joel a *what-do-we-do-now* look as an image of him walking through the streets barefoot plays like a movie before my eyes.

He nudges me into the room and says, "It's okay. Some kids are probably trying them on."

We take our seats on sofas and chairs. A mixture of pleasure and pride shines in the children's eyes as they serve our meal on rimmed metal plates. Nanda tells us it is mutton dal bhat. I stay away from the mutton which looks like peeled-back knuckles with bits of meat attached. The crunch I hear coming from Nanda as she begins to chew doesn't help.

"This is so good," she says as she picks up another piece with her fingers and crunches away.

I glance at Joel and see him struggling with a mouthful of mutton that won't go down and can't be spit out. Desperation does a slow dance across his eyes as he keeps a pleasant expression, almost a smile, on his face. I consider being a vegetarian for the rest of the trip.

Dal bhat, a Nepali staple of lentils cooked in buttery water (dhal) and rice (bhat), is fine without the mutton. Nanda demonstrates how to eat it using her fingers to massage the mixture into a ball and convey it to her mouth. I try the technique, but decide to perfect it later. I switch to a fork, thankful one is provided for unpracticed westerners.

A boy cleaning his plate on the orphanage rooftop after lunch was served.

Nanda glances at her watch and says, "It's 3:30. I have kept you here with my children a long time. I hope you like them. Now it is time for me to help you plan your visit to Kathmandu. Come. Let's go to my travel agency office. It's not far from here."

Thankfully, Joel's shoes have reappeared. Where they were remains a mystery; perhaps they brought fun to someone.

We leave the security of the building and re-enter the streets. We cross a wide street, its fast-moving vehicles make it more terrifying than the narrow ones.

"This wide street is new. Many accidents happen here. We Nepali are used to the small streets. We don't know how to drive on the new ones."

That bumps my heart rate up another notch.

Along the way, Nanda tells us, "My American friends will take the children they sponsor to shop for clothes. We may see them in Thamel where we are going."

Nanda's eyes betray something other than joy with this revelation.

"My American friends are good people; they raise money to help me care for the children. But, when they give gifts to the children they sponsor, how do the other children feel? When they pay for one child to go to a special school, it's not fair to the others. This is a problem for me. I would like the money they give to be for *all* the children. I have to raise the children to live in Nepal, to have the skills they need to get good job here."

I don't know what to say. I sneak a glance at Joel who looks as uncomfortable in his silence as I feel. I imagine how hurt I would be if I were a child left behind as other children went on a shopping spree. I search my mind to understand the conflicting ways of thinking that challenge Nanda and her American board. Americans pride themselves in individualism and cultivate the individual as much as, if not more than, the community. I can see Nanda embraces the whole more than its parts. The tension between her and her board must be great.

My focus shifts as we enter Thamel, the tourist area, with narrow winding streets lined with open-air shops and occasional restaurants buried among them. Cars share the walking space with us. We turn right and stop at a dark stairway sandwiched between two stores. A man sits on the bottom step. No words, just a brief but steady stare from Nanda and the man is gone. Three floors later we arrive at Nanda's office, slip off our shoes, and enter. A fortyish, dark haired man in a white, short-sleeve shirt and khaki trousers comes from behind his desk to greet us.

"This is Lok, my partner. He will take care of you."

I am bewildered at the handoff; I thought she was going to give us personal care. I learn later that Nanda has an arrangement with Lok that for every client she brings to him, he will donate a portion of the money he earns to care for her children at the orphanage.

By now the absence of sleep has softened my brain. I sink into a chair and go through the motions of listening to Lok's soft voice as he asks questions from the opposite side of his desk and Joel answers from his chair alongside mine. I agree to everything they say. We will spend two days touring Kathmandu. Lok names the places. I ask him to spell them as I attempt to write them down. On my third attempt, he has pity on me, takes my piece of paper and writes the names for me.

We are almost done when I remember something Nanda had mentioned on the airplane.

"What is Poon Hill?" I ask Lok.

"It's in the Himalayas. Would you like to do a trek?"

"No!" shoots out of my mouth as a simultaneous "Yes" drifts from Joel's.

The panic I feel must show on my face. Joel turns to me and says, "We don't have to do a trek. Let's just hear what Lok has to say."

I know Joel; I know his patience in letting things come around to his way. I realize I have just dangled one foot over a cliff, but my other foot is securely nailed to concrete by my fear of death, falls, and fractured bones.

Lok looks from my face to Joel's and doesn't move or say anything until Joel gives a nod and I manage a silent stare. He tells us about the trek to Poon Hill—a short trek, five days, six to ten hours of hiking each day. Joel's eyes gleam, mine shoot *no-way-we're-doing-this* bullets his way.

"I assume you're in good shape for this," Lok asks more than says.

I don't answer.

We sign an agreement for a two-day tour of Kathmandu to begin on Monday, reserve Sunday for sleep, and leave the trek to dangle in the air like a sparkling saber.

Nanda Kulu in Thamel, the tourist shopping area.

Chapter Five

# BODY AND SOUL

*Sunday, September 4*

I make peace with my jet-lagged body, sleep late, and convince Joel to join me in a couples' massage. He feels a little awkward slipping into the silky boxer shorts a pretty masseuse gives him to protect his modesty; but gets annoyed by the giggles exchanged between my masseuse and his after the massage is underway. He'll seek retribution from me for his having gone along with my suggestion without complaining, but I'm not going to worry about that now.

I awake from a post-massage nap full of energy and ready to go. Warm sunlight flows into our room as Joel sleeps on. I pop out of bed a few times, rising with the urge to do something, but stop short and slip back under the covers when I can't figure out what to do with myself. I begin to wonder what I will do for two weeks. Joel's soft breathing and contented face look like he knows what he'll do; but I don't think I want to spend the next twelve days watching him in a peaceful, somnolent state. Sleep is his favorite thing to do when he is not a machine set on automatic with no stop button in sight.

There is a limit to how many massages I can get. The indoor pool is large and lovely, but there is also a limit to how much swimming and sitting-by-the-pool-reading I can do. I don't play golf. There are shops with colorful Pashmina shawls and turquoise jewelry, but Joel would set a limit on how much of that I could do.

I sneak a peek at Joel and hold my breath, afraid somehow he will hear my thoughts as I begin to make a mental list comparing comfort at the resort with trekking through the mountains. Joel awakes as I finish considering the pros and cons of *Plan A* to go trekking and *Plan B* to stay put:

| PLAN A<br>GO TREKKING | PLAN B<br>STAY PUT |
| --- | --- |
| Sleeping bags | Comfy bed |
| Tea rooms with basic Nepali food | Restaurants with an international menu |
| Leeches on you if it rains | No leeches |
| Six to ten hours of hiking eacl day | Ninety-minute massages |
| Sometimes a bathroom in your room | Large bathroom, hot shower |
| Showers? (I'm afraid to ask) | Swimming pool, sauna with more showers |

Trekking would mean eight days away from the resort. We would get back just in time to spend a day cleaning up before catching a plane back to Texas. Plan B—Stay Put—is what my body and soul are pleading with me to choose. I can hear them saying, "What are you nuts? In the last few years you haven't hiked in mountains for more than six hours. The one time you did, your legs gave out an hour before the hike did and you asked someone to shoot you to put you out of your misery."

It would be smart to obey my rational inner voices, but I'm not handling relaxation very well. I might go crazy if I spend two weeks surrounded by luxury. With *Plan A, Go Trekking*, Joel would get to see the Himalayas up close and I would get to complain.

I turn to Joel and say, "I've been thinking. I might get bored if I stay at the resort for two weeks. I don't know yet, but maybe we should go trekking."

I'm startled by how quickly this lump of laziness loses all grogginess. He's out of bed and on the phone with Lok before I have a chance to buffer my tentative nod of approval with more *ifs* and *maybes*. All I hear is, "Yes. Yes. Tuesday night. Gokarna Resort? Eight o'clock? Great."

I make no attempt to hide the fear that's pushing my eyes out of their sockets as my reasoned calm converts to mild terror.

"We don't have to go. We haven't committed to anything. You can change your mind," Joel tells me, ever considerate, ever patient. That makes it harder, but not impossible, to say, "No."

Ebullience defines Joel as he strides along the hall and bounces down the steps on the way to the dining room. I look like a slug that crawled out of the bottom of a fish tank. The waiter must think I'm sick; he brings a cup of tea made from locally grown basil leaves. With halting English and hand motions, he tells me, "Good for health, especially stomach."

My stomach is fine. The spice in the foods I've been eating for breakfast, lunch, and dinner could kill anything trying to grow inside. I have had so many Indian, Tibetan, and Nepali curry-based dishes since I arrived that I'm starting to sweat curry.

The waiter stands by with an expectant smile until I sip the delicately delicious tea and say, "Mmmm. This is so good. Thank you." I succumb to the tea's steamy comfort. It dulls, but doesn't erase, the image of a trekking saber hovering over me.

Chapter Six

# SPINNING WHEELS

*Monday, September 5*

It's nine o'clock in the morning and I'm in the lobby with Joel ready to meet our guide. I've had my usual breakfast— a sampling of everything set out on the Chinese, Indian, and Nepali buffet tables. When it comes to food, Joel shows some self-restraint: I possess none.

A delicately handsome man with dark eyes approaches. The smooth skin of his round face renders him ageless. "Hello, Mr. and Mrs. Deretchin," a slight question mark accompanies the near-perfect pronunciation of our last name. "My name is Shiva like the deity. I will be your guide for the next two days. Come, the car is waiting. We have lots of things to see today."

The soft-spoken man dressed in a crisp, white shirt and dark slacks leads us to a subcompact car. The interior, decorated with crocheted white doilies, is immaculate. Shiva slips into the front passenger seat, a driver waits for Joel and me to settle in.

"We will start at the far end of Kathmandu and work our way back," Shiva tells us.

I'm not surprised that our tour will begin on the other side of Kathmandu. I have come to accept the daily forty-five minute no-contact-bumper-car ride as inevitable.

I peer through the space between the driver's seat and Shiva's. From that vantage point I can see out the windshield or watch the driver—I choose the driver. My eyes focus on his toasted-almond arms that move with the quick confidence of youth. He weaves, passes, shifts, answers his cell phone, and speaks in spurts to Shiva as I cower in the back seat and breathe my way into a mind-preserving trance.

Joel interrupts my near-meditative state with, "Look at that!" My head whips left just in time to see a diminutive woman half-lifting, half-coaxing a gray goat that is almost as big as she is onto the top of a bus the size of a minivan. Inside, riders sit shoulder-to-shoulder along the walls of the van, waiting for the woman to complete her task. The image of the uncooperative goat and the passengers barely registers as we zip past into more traffic, more people, and more movement. Relative calm prevails as we reach the wider, less congested areas at the far side of town.

We turn onto a street where women sit on the sidewalk on blankets outside a temple. Their frocks of golden-orange, peacock blue, and yellow-green trump the colors of the fruits, nuts, and vegetables lying on cloths or in small bins. Patterned umbrellas in pinks, blues, and reds shade the women from the early-morning sunlight. Already intense, it heats the stone sidewalk that surrounds them. By noon even shadows will seek refuge from the sun.

Shiva asks, "Would you like to see this temple? It was built by Tibetan Buddhists who settled here after the Chinese entered Tibet. It's not on the tour, but we can stop here if you'd like. The temple is about ten years old."

The driver pulls over and lets us out. I walk no more than a few paces when a short burst of angry words flies out of the mouth of one of the sidewalk women. I turn to see the object of her fury. A light brown monkey the size of a four-year-old child bolts from the scene of the crime clutching a stolen handful of the woman's peanuts. The mischievous look on his face says he'll be back for more.

Just outside the temple grounds I climb several steps and enter a prayer wheel house through a rectangular concrete opening. It's trimmed with carvings painted pink, yellow, green, and blue. Inside, a giant prayer wheel—a cylindrical drum on a spindle inscribed with a mantra in Sanskrit—has small versions of itself encircling its base. The small ones spin freely with a light touch of the hand. Spinning the wheels is supposed to be as good as saying the prayer each one contains. I spin half-a-dozen prayers not knowing what I'm praying when a Buddhist monk in an orange robe and maroon wrap enters. I slip away, abandoning my curiosity, leaving the sanctity of the prayer wheels to him.

I trip several times on my black, tiered skirt as I climb the steps to the Buddhist holy place. I do away with regard for Nepali modesty, gather the skirt in front of me and resume the climb. An array of temples and shrines spans the sun-drenched grounds. Intricate carvings in bright blues, yellows, pinks, greens, and reds adorn the structures, which are lavishly trimmed with gold. I marvel at the capacity of the displaced Buddhist community to build something so elaborate and meaningful to their beliefs and culture, especially in this century which shuns people-intensive labor in favor of speed, simplification, and mechanization.

"How many Tibetan Buddhists are there in Nepal?" I ask.

"About 25,000. Maybe more. It's hard to count. Not all that come here register," replies Shiva.

Buddhist temple built at the beginning of the 21<sup>st</sup> Century.

Joel busies himself taking pictures from every angle of every structure while I walk around touching every surface I can reach. After a while Shiva says, "Now I will take you to see Swayambhunath, an ancient Buddhist temple. It is also called 'Monkey Temple.' It got that name when students from the United States hung out there smoking pot in the 1960s. They couldn't pronounce the temple's name so they looked around, saw a lot of monkeys, and called it 'Monkey Temple.'"

The driver appears with the car ready to chauffer us to the next sight. We've never had a chauffeured, guided tour before—this is nice!

Swayambhunath, we learn, is a Buddhist holy site revered by Hindus as well as Buddhists. It was built in the fifth century and is a much larger complex than the one we just left. The expanse of statuary and structures that appear on multiple levels separated by flights of steps causes me to redefine "temple" as a complex rather than a single structure.

We make it past artisans displaying their work in booths lined up side-by-side near the entry, but can't escape the ones that troll the grounds. I won't be able to leave Joel alone—he doesn't know how to say no to anyone hawking goods.

Monkey at Swayambhunath Temple, also known as "Monkey Temple."

Shrine at Swayambhunath Temple.

I barely get past several monkeys and the first shrine when an artisan comes up to me with a small sculpture of a family of elephants held in the palm of his hand. Intricate symbols and patterns are etched into layers of dark resin to reveal red, bone-colored, and white lines that form a delicate design.

"Miss, would you like to buy this. I carved it myself. Look. Very fine work. Sixty-five dollars."

"No thank you." I gather my skirt and set out to climb the 365 steps leading to the Swayambhunath stupa, a holy shrine encapsulating Buddhist beliefs.

"I make you a good price. Fifty dollars. Look. Lots of work," the artisan follows me as I begin the ascent.

"It's beautiful, but I'm not buying anything today."

"Forty dollars."

"No. I see you did a lot of work. It's beautiful and you should get the sixty-five dollars you want for it."

"Thirty-five."

Along comes Joel just as the artisan lowers his price again. He brings with him another artisan with a sculpture of a man etched similarly, but not as finely executed.

"Louise, take a look at this," the plea in Joel's eye says, "Can we buy this?" He knows I am still on my austerity kick.

Now I have two artisans standing near me with my husband on their side. I give in and select the family of elephants and feel guilty for paying so little, but not willing to pass up a deal.

At the top of the stairs, we come to the Swayambhunath stupa, a vertical compilation of religiously significant symbols that are stacked on a concrete dome base more than two stories high. Piercing, painted eyes dominate a square structure that sits immediately above the dome. A Tibetan symbol for a lotus flower crowns the stupa. Prayer flags, hung in repeated patterns of blue, white, red, green, and yellow, flutter in the breeze along cables that stretch from the stupa's top to anchor points at the corners of its base.

"What do the flags symbolize," I ask Shiva.

"The blue is for the sky, white for the wind. Red is for fire, green for water and yellow for earth." He pauses then adds, "The balance of the five elements brings health and harmony. The flags also promote peace, compassion, and wisdom."

Swayambhunath stupa: The concrete dome near the base houses precious relics and writings.

Shiva tells us, "The stupa represents the stages of enlightenment. The four sides are the four qualities of mind needed to attain enlightenment: love, compassion, joy, and equanimity. The lotus flower at the top represents enlightenment, the ultimate level of perfection."

Shiva continues, "To attain enlightenment is to become a Buddha."

A Buddha is a person that has achieved enlightenment? I toss that around in my mind and come to understand that there are multiple Buddhas rather than one Buddha with multiple names. I turn to Shiva and say, "The eyes are intriguing. What do they represent?"

"They are called 'Buddha Eyes,' sometimes 'Wisdom Eyes.' They face north, east, south and west to represent all-seeing. The small dot between the eyes is called 'the third eye.' It is the symbol of spiritual awakening."

"And the shape that looks like a question mark or a nose?"

"That's the Tibetan numeral one. It stands for the unity of all things."

I meander through the concrete spaces people-watching, examining the structures that cover this sacred area, and enjoying the quiet that floats on the breeze. Children, alongside parents, pray or sit by temples and shrines. Dogs and monkeys roam freely; food is set out for them. The flow of people and animals, conversations, and clicks from cameras fail to interrupt the peacefulness that permeates the setting.

I enter an open air shrine and see a man praying before a framed, glass-covered image of a person, maybe a Buddha, hung on the wall. He bends at the waist, lowers himself to the floor, then pushes up from a push-up position and repeats this several times in rapid succession. I stare silently in awe of his strength. To my right a woman prays in the same way.

Joel calls me to an overlook. "There's Kathmandu Valley," he says pointing to what could pass for Los Angeles' sister city with its sprawl and mountain-trapped smog. My eyes sweep the landscape as Joel points out wealthy parts of the city, parks, and roads we have been on. I marvel at his ability to observe and remember things.

Kathmandu Valley from Swayambhunath Temple.

I turn from the view and see a collection of miniature sculptures that resemble tombstones crowded into a corner a few feet from the Swayambhunath stupa.

Shiva tells me, "Those are small stupas built for family members who have passed. If one is built for a dead relative, it changes a suffering rebirth into a fortunate rebirth."

Stupas built for deceased loved ones to insure a fortunate rebirth.

We mingle a while longer with the tourists and pilgrims who have journeyed to this holy site. Today, the latter outnumber the former. Shiva quietly signals that it is time to move on to the next site.

Going down the steps to the exit, I wonder if there is a deity that protects ill-informed tourists from the perils of long skirts. The bottom tier of my black skirt slips under my heel and tugs at the elastic waistband which threatens to expose something worse than a little leg. I reach behind, bunch the skirt in my hand once again, and continue down.

On the way out, we pass a booth with the artisan from whom I bought the elephant carving. He calls me over to show me how much more delicately carved my purchase is than the others on display.

"See. You have a beautiful one! I just started this one last week. It will be beautiful, too."

I take mine out of my purse and examine the bottom for the artisan's signature. There is none.

"Would you sign this for me?"

"Yes, Miss. How do you spell your name?"

"No, no. Not my name," I say with a smile. "I would like to have your name on it. You are the artist."

"Ah," he says with a broad smile and a little confusion on his face.

He prints "Afta Budim" and explains he didn't have room for his whole name on the bottom of one elephant foot, so he put the "im" on another one to the left of the first.

## Chapter Seven

# PALACES AND KINGDOMS

*Still Monday, September 5*

It's not yet midday when we head to our third stop. The driver gets too close to a pedestrian and nicks her elbow with the side view mirror. She returns a stern glance as she holds her elbow up to check for damage and, without a word, continues down the street.

I watch the girl glide past as Shiva launches into a history of the area. His soft voice competes with the sound of car horns and the kinetic chaos that surrounds us.

"Before the unification of Nepal, there were three Kingdoms in Kathmandu Valley. The three Durbar Squares we will visit are where the royal families built their palaces, temples, and shrines." My mind turns off as Shiva travels through dates and names. The last bit of information I retain is that the unification took place in the seventeen hundreds.

"Do royalty live in the Durbar Squares?" I ask as I envision a crowned and caped queen strolling outside a palace. The heat and humidity that wilts my own clothes strips the cape from the image.

"Maybe some royalty spends time at the palace, but they have moved to other homes—newer, more modern," answers Shiva.

We arrive at Kathmandu Durbar Square and my eyes dance to an unfamiliar rhythm as I take in the visual treat. Pagodas I would expect to see nestled in the shadows of tree-covered mountains are bathed in uninterrupted sunlight and surrounded by paved pathways and small plazas. The darkness of the structures contrasts sharply with the bright colors of the Buddhist temple we visited early in the day; bright sunshine mediates the darkness.

"Pagodas were created in Nepal," Shiva tells me drawing my attention away from the visual and back to the historical.

A soft smile spreads across his face as he says, "Others copied it from us."

He points to the red ruffled material that workers hang along the edges of roofs. "The temples are being prepared for Indra Jatra—a festival in honor of Indra, the god of rain and thunder."

Kathmandu Durbar Square temples and shrines.

I think about my Texas friend Sandra's warning to avoid being in Nepal during festivals, "Everything shuts down. You can't do anything or get any services." I brush the thought aside; I don't have to worry, our trip is tucked between festivals.

I gaze at the cylindrical supports carved into the shape of gods and goddesses that connect the overhangs of multi-tiered pagodas to their brick walls. Intricate wood carvings frame the windows: peacocks for peace and love; serpents for good luck and protection; dragons for prosperity and peace. Lattice work covers the would-be openings to windows rendering them visually impenetrable from where we stand.

Kathmandu Durbar Square: Carved palace window typical
of the carving found on palaces and temples.

"The windows let you see out, but you can't see in."
Shiva pauses and then says, "They keep all good things
inside and bad things out."

The square is filled with Hindu and Buddhist
pilgrims mostly from Nepal and India with which Nepal
shares an open border. The scene is one of peaceful
enjoyment rather than the solemnity and formality my
western-self associates with holy places. People sit and
stand on temple steps and balconies; dots of color from
their clothing interrupt the starkness of the dark structures.

Luscious blues, oranges, pinks, and reds of the
women's saris grace the plaza. Single plaited braids like a
woven arrows point down the women's backs almost to

their waists. Men dressed in western clothes appear demure by comparison in their pale blues, pinks, and tans.

I turn to see Shiva make a motion to stop Joel from doing something, but the look on Shiva's face as he lowers his outstretched arm says he's too late. A holy man dressed in a saffron colored robe with a gold headpiece worthy of Queen Elizabeth's millinery collection has Joel engaged in conversation. Round, rimless glasses are barely visible against the holy man's painted-red face. A foot-long, gray beard moves up and down as he talks to his willing listener. I can tell by Joel's kindly smile that he doesn't understand a word the man is saying, but there's no need for words; the body language of solicitation is universal.

Joel reaches into his pocket and extracts change to give to the holy man unaware that his generosity is creating a commotion. The expression on Joel's face changes from warmth to puzzlement as passersby converge on him like spokes of a wheel and admonish him with a shake of the head or a wave of the hand and a stern "No."

"Some holy men make a lot of money from tourists," Shiva says and then adds with a shrug of his shoulders. "Some Nepalis don't like that."

With an apology written across his face, Joel lets the change slide back into his pocket. But, when the crowd's attention shifts elsewhere, I see him slip money into the hand of the holy man.

Shiva leads us past more temples and then through a doorway into a small courtyard with carved windows and doors.

"This is the House of the Kumari. She is a living goddess and is worshipped by Buddhists and Hindus," Shiva begins. He tells us she is chosen from among children who live in poverty, but doesn't mention she must be a member of the lowest caste, the untouchables.

The religious tradition of worshipping a child-goddess began when a king who was enthralled by the goddess Teleju angered her. For punishment, the goddess told the king that she would no longer appear to him as a beautiful woman, but as a child; and this child would be found among people living in the lowliest of slums—a people and place detested by royalty.

"How is the Kumari chosen?" I ask.

"It's a very complicated process. A committee of Buddhist priests and the royal astrologer search for young girls between the age of four and seven who meet thirty-two attributes of perfection: dainty hands and feet, well-shaped teeth, none of which have been lost, a soft and clear voice. The child's hair and eyes must be black, her body unblemished, and her horoscope must match the king's. When the priests believe they have found the child that can be the Kumari, she must spend the night in a dark room with bloody animal heads. If the child shows fear, the search continues. Only a child that shows calm can be the Kumari."

Shiva continues as Joel and I gaze at the house that encloses the courtyard on all four sides.

"She is brought to The House of the Kumari when she is between the ages of four and seven. A ceremony is performed that lets the goddess Taleju enter the child's body."

"Is the Kumari a symbol of the goddess or really the goddess?" I ask.

"She *is* the goddess."

I feel as if the equivalent of a lump in my throat ripples through my mind as I take in Shiva's reply.

"How long does the Kumari live here?"

"Until her first bleed. If she is unlucky and gets a scratch that bleeds before then, she changes back to an ordinary human being and a search for a new Kumari begins."

I listen to Shiva and peer at the windows that keep the outside out and hope to detect a movement that might be the child-goddess peering at us from within.

"Is she here now?" I ask.

"Yes. She remains here except for festivals and rituals. During Indra Jatra, the festival they are preparing for now, she will be carried into public in a chariot—her feet are not allowed to touch the ground as long as she is the Kumari. Thousands of people will come to see and be blessed by her; even a glance from the Kumari will mean good luck. The king, and now the president of Nepal, will also come to be blessed to ensure the success of their rule."

"Does her family live with her?"

"She has caretakers the government provides. The family can visit."

I imagine myself as a child kept inside a house with caretakers who cater to my every need, but no siblings. I ask, "Does she have any friends her own age to play with?"

"Friends come to play."

When I ask about her education, Shiva tells me that she has books and teachers.

"What happens to the Kumari after she leaves this house?"

"She goes back to her home."

Later I learn that she'll return to the slum from which she came, uneducated or undereducated, a stranger to her family, lacking social skills, and will have difficulty marrying because of a superstition that any man who marries a former Kumari will die young. The return must be a bitter pill for an adolescent to swallow after being worshipped as a goddess from when she was barely beyond toddlerhood. I wonder how the family deals with the high honor of having their child selected to be the embodiment of a goddess and the mortal stranger that is returned to them.

It's one o'clock. Two Buddhist holy sites and a Durbar Square since we started out this morning. My head is overstuffed and my stomach is empty. The heat and humidity have silenced my curiosity. I begin to think that a hike in the Himalayas might be easier.

"We will go to Patan Durbar Square."

I almost sink to the sidewalk before Shiva adds, "First we will have some lunch."

We walk down a block-long street that is narrow even by Nepali standards. Every inch is packed with people, shops, and merchandise. There is no room for a car, although I would not be surprised if one managed to squeeze its way through.

Just beyond lies a sun-washed plaza and, not far from there, two broad flights of stairs lead to a rooftop restaurant, ice tea, and breaded fried chicken. I suspect from the menu that Shiva has no confidence in our ability to eat Nepali food.

Cooled down and refueled, we walk to Patan Durbar Square, the seat of the second kingdom. Like the first, it is filled with people and red-ruffled pagodas; but its balance of form and space makes it especially pleasing. Joel's camera clicks away.

Patan Durbar Square.

The sound of singing and drums draws our attention to a procession. Men and women carry trays of treats. Girls that appear to be between the ages of seven and nine wear ankle-length, red dresses that shimmer with gold. Red-orange paint spans each one's forehead.

"They are wearing wedding dresses," Shiva tells us. "This is the first of three marriages, this one to the god Vishnu, the protector of the universe. When they are about twelve, they will wed the sun. Their third marriage will be to their real husbands."

Young girls prepared for their marriage to the god Vishnu.

As this procession thins out, another follows. Carried on the shoulders of six men, an elderly woman, seated in a litter covered with multicolored ribbons and beads, is raised above the crowd.

"She is very old. They are honoring her."

How lovely to honor the elderly. I think about back home where many elderly are treated as economic burdens, intrusions on busy lives, and where financially strapped healthcare systems consider classifying the elderly as disposable. They don't label them "disposable," they just say it may not be in the economic interest of the system to treat them. It's no wonder so many of us try so desperately to stay young.

Five-thirty finds us back at the resort. My head is filled with a plethora of images, gods, goddesses, and history. After a day of tantalizing colors, I can't resist stepping into a shop that has a rainbow of pashminas stacked neatly on shelves. The lack of clutter is almost as appealing as the softness of the shawls woven from the wool of Pashmina goats that roam at high altitudes in the Himalayas of Nepal. I buy four—one for each of my two daughters and two for me. The proportion of gift-giving feels just about right.

Chapter Eight

# Thirteen Steps

*Tuesday, September 6*

"Do you have your passports?" Shiva greets us with a smile and a reminder.

I'm not smiling—the passports bring us one step closer to a trek. My stomach clenches as my mind teases, "You can still back out." I feel as if I'm standing on the edge of a precipice and tilting forward. I wish Joel would grab me, but the passports in his hand are like an index finger pushing against my spine. Sullen, I prepare for another day of traffic and sites. Shiva is talking, but my head is too full of my own thoughts to listen to what he says. I know from the itinerary that we'll start at the stupa in Boudhanath, an area known as "Little Tibet." That's all I care to know for now.

The almond-skinned driver with quick reflexes is with us again. I don't see his face or know his name, but do know his arms; for hours I've watched them shift gears, steer in and out of traffic, and reach for his cell phone. Today is no different.

He pulls over and lets us out. We walk through a tall arch, pay an entry fee, and there it sits squarely in the middle of its own little kingdom, a stupa of enormous proportions. As I stare at it, dynamic tension holds me in place, neither sucking me in nor pushing me away. I'm unable to tear my eyes from it.

The concrete base on which the dome of the stupa sits is the density and size of a huge war bunker, the dome itself, the size of a planetarium. Buddha eyes painted on the cube above the dome watch with a sternness that betrays an underlying softness and understanding. Spinning prayer wheels embedded in a six-foot, stucco wall that encircles the stupa are set in motion with flick of a wrist by passersby.

At the entrance to Boudhanath Stupa, Boudhanades, Nepal.

Boudhanath Stupa.

I'm barely aware of what Shiva is saying until he points high up on the stupa and says, "The steps represent the thirteen steps to Nirvana."

I count the steps that taper upward to make sure there really are thirteen and think, "This is the closest I will ever get to Nirvana."

When I finally free my eyes from the stupa, I become transfixed by the colors surrounding me. Two wide bands of pavement encircle the stupa wall—the inner of stone, the outer of pea gravel. On the outer edge of the paths are clothes made of brilliant blues, reds, and oranges that hang outside shops with open fronts. I want to scoop up every bit of color in my arms.

"Give me the camera," I whisper to Joel with urgency as I tug at the camera strap on his shoulder. Engrossed in what Shiva is telling him, he barely notices me. He could be handing off the camera to a stranger.

I swing around and move the camera from point-to-point and try to capture what I see in the view finder, but I can only photograph one corner at a time. I can't photograph the feeling of unconstrained joy and excitement that runs through me. Disappointed, I turn back ready to listen. I tune in in time to catch Shiva say, ". . . built in the 1300s . . ." And then, "It's the largest stupa in Nepal and the holiest Tibetan Buddhist site outside Tibet."

At the top of the steps leading to the base of the dome are two men with buckets by their feet. One passes a bucket to the other who flings its content onto the dome. The yellow liquid creates a perfectly shaped arch, easily twice the man's height. He heaves a second bucket and its contents follow the exact path as the first intensifying the yellow of the arch.

"He's painting lotus petals to honor someone." Shiva tells us.

One perfect petal at a time is created by the painter's perfect toss. When he finishes, petals will encircle the dome. A ceremonial washing of the dome to remove the paint will occur before someone pays to have another person honored.

I join other strollers along the path—Tibetan, Indian, Nepali men, women and children, monks and nuns—that form a vibrant patchwork of beauty. The colors of their clothing vie with the vivid colors of fabrics hanging outside the shops. Until now I had regarded my white skirt and bright pink blouse as colorful.

I step into a dimly lighted temple, every inch of which is covered in swirls of bold colors that form symbols for the earth, enlightenment, the interconnectedness of everything in the world, and compassion. The swirls of paint look like a fire storm around the sculptures of deities. Set among the decorated forms stands a large, framed photograph of the Dalai Lama. The flatness of the photograph looks out of place in such a sculpted environment; but I understand the limitations of the medium and the importance of the tribute.

The sound of cymbals draws me outside into the bright sunlight. Monks lead a procession of men and women around the prayer-wheel wall that encircles the stupa. A white cloth the length and width of a bolt of fabric, stretches from hand to hand along the procession and terminates at a litter carried on the shoulder of several men. The litter is draped with white, blue, yellow, and green fabric that covers its top and sides and blocks any view of its contents.

Shiva tells us, "It is a funeral procession. The Tibetan community has come out to honor someone who has died. The men are carrying the body. Later, they will take the body to be cremated."

Boudhanath, Nepal. Tibetan funeral procession.

I remain silent as I try to picture the position of the dead person in what looks like a four-foot square box. The body must be folded into it; certainly there is not enough room to lay it out as we would do. I learn later that at the time of death, the family washes the body and wraps it with cloth that binds it in the fetal position.

The procession passes. Movement that had ceased resumes. I take a breath and continue along with everyone else.

Shiva leads us up the steps to the base of the stupa's dome. Through lines of fluttering prayer flags hung from the stupa, I look at the restaurants, stores, and guest houses that surround it. The Buddha eyes above me survey the stupa's little kingdom and make everything inside me feel so right, so balanced, so complete that I wish I could stay here for a long time if not forever.

Boudhanath. Prayer flags strung from buildings that encircle the stupa.

We descend and continue around the stupa along the paved path. A moment of truth comes as we pass an outfitters shop.

Joel looks at me with an inquiring eye. I say, "I can't climb a mountain in this skirt."

We back up a few steps and look at trekking gear to supplement the boots and walking sticks we brought with us to hike around Kathmandu. I prefer doing almost anything to shopping, but when I see that everything is one-fourth the price we would pay in the United States, the bargain-hunter in me goes on full alert. The prices are enough to push me over the edge. I start to shop fully aware that I'm sealing my fate; a trek will happen.

There are no women's hiking pants, so I try on men's. I do battle with the privacy curtain that wraps around me and bulges wherever I bend or poke. The men's size small refuses to go on my body; I ask for a medium. I can zip it up.

"You're not going to be able to do a trek in those. Try a larger size." Joel's bluntness stabs me.

"Men's large! You have to be kidding." How much breakfast have I been eating?

"Just try the large."

Back into the curtain. The pants pull up with ease.

"That's better." So he says.

"They're too big," I say in protest as I pull at the loose fabric at my legs.

"No they're not. They're flattering on you."

"They're baggy. Let me put the mediums on again."

Into the curtain and out I come. "See? These fit better."

Shiva weighs in, "Turn around."

With my head twisted over my shoulder, I see him take a studied look at my buttocks and feel the blood rush to my face.

"No. The other ones," he says without equivocation.

I give in, but don't like it.

Joel spots something and says, "Come look at these."

"What are they?"

"Head lamps. They might come in handy if we have to hike in the dark."

Two tops, a duffle bag, two headlamps, and the hiking pants later we head to the car and our next stop, Pashupati. Thousands of pilgrims travel to this holy site each year—most are from India. For Hindus, it is one of the holiest sites.

The Pashupatinath Temple is off limits to anyone who is not Hindu. I strain my neck to peek inside but mostly see men, women, and children slip their shoes off and on as they enter and exit the temple. Outside, cows and monkeys wander freely among pilgrims and holy men. Pashupati, I learn later, is the Lord of the Animals.

Shiva leads us to the Bagmati River on the edge of the temple grounds. Maybe it's the sudden grayness of the day, the smoke-dulled air, or the contrast with the bold brightness of Boudhanath Stupa that makes this area look joyless and still. Small, concrete platforms, some with piles of wood burning in the center, line the side of the river we stand on. The other side has steps leading up from the water with a smattering of people seated on them; many sit alone.

Shiva points to his right and says, "This side is for public cremations. To the left is for private ones. The ashes of the deceased are swept into the river. They are returned to the river. The river is life."

I glance at the river and see that it is very dark. A woman sweeps rubbish and a black plastic bag into it. I don't say anything to Shiva about what I see; I prefer to think of the river as representing the life to which the deceased are returned.

"Both Hindus and Buddhists are cremated at this site," Shiva adds.

A funeral pyre is being prepared for one body, another is still burning. Flowers follow ashes floating downstream from yet another body.

A man places something that looks like straw on a body being cremated. I ask Shiva what the man is doing.

"That's to keep the ashes from blowing away," he replies.

The stillness and simplicity of the process befits a private goodbye and the return of the deceased to another life.

Shiva nods toward the people the opposite side of the river. "They are performing ceremonies to honor their dead ancestors and relatives. It is important to honor them. If your ancestors are not happy, you will have a hard life."

We linger silently for a while, and then move on.

Pashupati. Funeral pyres along the Bagmati River.

Ashes swept from a funeral pyre and flowers left for the
deceased float together down the left side of the river.

A sense of urgency replaces the casual calm I am
used to seeing in Shiva. He tells us that Lok, our travel
agent, has given him an assignment: Get passport photos
made for permits to trek. I feel as if a well-executed
conspiracy among Joel, Lok, and Shiva has just played out.
An hour later, a handoff of the photos and copies of our
passports is made and we are on our way to Bhaktapur
Durbar Square, the site of the third kingdom in Kathmandu.
Wisely, Shiva brings us to a rooftop restaurant immediately
inside the square. It gives me a chance to settle my wits
after the passport photo-taking brought the reality of the
trek to the surface.

The large square looks big and empty. There are just a handful of people wandering around.

"It's not tourist season yet. That begins in October and November. Then every place we have been to will be crowded with tourists," Shiva says.

The broad, open courtyard rimmed with intricately carved buildings, combines peace with beauty. I glance at it; Joel becomes transfixed.

"This is the most beautiful site we've seen," slips almost inaudibly from Joel's lips. "It's a classic plaza with a big open space and buildings on its periphery."

This is the place where he could stay for a long, long time. Its orderliness must give his eye a rest. I, on the other hand, still have my mind filled with this morning's images and have little room for more. As Joel clicks away with his camera, I meander aimlessly looking at the carvings, intrigued by the windows.

Entry to Bhaktapur Durbar Square.

As we leave Bhaktapur Durbar Square, a hawker attaches himself to Joel. He holds a foot-long, sheathed Gurkha knife, its black handle and case decorated with brass symbols.

"I make this myself. Look. It is beautiful."

"No thank you," says Joel.

"I make a good price."

The price comes down with each step Joel takes. He stops saying, "No thank you," and the hawker begins bargaining with himself. I see Joel begin to weaken; his eyes are lingering on the unsheathed knife, its shiny blade classically bent at a ten-degree angle. I give him the last nudge he needs to purchase one when I say, "They would make nice gifts for our sons-in-law." He buys two, one for each son-in-law, and later regrets not having bought one for himself.

As we leave the square, we pass shops that sell carvings. I tug at Joel's arm and pull him inside one that's carvings look particularly well done. We buy a wooden replica of the latticed windows we saw in the Durbar Squares. It's only twenty inches wide and twelve inches high, but, just as the palace and temple windows keep good things inside, the replica will hold good memories of this intriguing place inside.

More has been packed into today than into any week I have spent elsewhere and it's not over yet. At dinner in the resort dining room, Joel says to me, "Why are you so afraid to do the trek? I can't believe you walked on a narrow ledge with a 700-foot drop in Sedona and that didn't scare you in the least. But you're afraid of a trek!"

It's true. Bushwhacking with a guide in Sedona, Arizona several years ago the guide pointed to a cave dwelling accessed from a ledge. No more than four-inches wide, the ledge was too narrow to put down a foot. I inched sideways on tiptoe with the front of my body against the mountain, arms spread, and hands sliding along the smooth rock surface. The guide moved just ahead of me and uttered encouragement. His index finger pressed against my spine was the only support I had as I traversed the 100-foot distance to the abandoned cave. The reward was a spectacular view of sky, mountains, and cactus-filled land seen through two, stoned-framed openings from inside the dwelling. Joel, who had assessed the danger and declined the invitation to the cave, waited in safety and contemplated becoming a widower.

Like Joel, I don't understand why I had no fear on the mountain ledge 700 feet up yet find at other times my knees buckle if I stand on something eighteen inches above ground level.

"We'll go at your pace. I'll walk behind you. Nothing's going to happen. You'll be okay," Joel says.

I wish I could believe him, but my mother's admonitions throughout my childhood, "You're going to fall. You'll get hurt," cut a groove into my psyche that's clawing its way to the surface now.

The many hikes I've taken over the years have convinced me I was never a mountain goat in a previous life. My feet have a penchant for finding loose rocks to step on; my narrow ankles twist easily; and my skinny wrists are not meant to break a fall. I have a permanent hole in my wrist cartilage as proof. It happened while I hiked on a trail in the Rocky Mountains five summers ago. I wish I could say it was a dramatic tumble, but it wasn't. The trail was buried in trees and had no drop-offs to worry about. Even with surgery, I still get sporadic, piercing pain in my ratchety left wrist.

Each time I have hiked since that fall, I have hiked with a level of fear that has been easy to bat down. But it's asking too much of me to bat down the fear that arises when I think about spending days in the Himalayas stumbling across ragged rocks, afraid to look up and afraid to look down.

We leave the dining room and meet Lok in the bar to sign a contract to trek. He and Joel order a drink; I refrain. We exchange papers, permits, and money for a five-day trek in the Annapurna Mountain Range of the Himalayas to view the high peaks from the top of Poon Hill. I think about the drag I'll be on Joel and the guide as they march with confidence into the wilderness and I trudge over rocks, pick my way carefully, and try to forestall the inevitable bone-breaking fall. I don't expect to come out of this in one piece.

Lok must see fear in my face because when the deal is done and he is about to leave, he pauses and with a kindly expression says, "When you go downhill, walk sideways, like this." With his feet turned sideways and moving in parallel, he demonstrates taking tiny steps. "Don't walk with your toes facing down the mountain." He adds, "And don't step back when you take pictures."

That does it! My insides collapse. My fragile decision to go along with this cockamamie idea shatters.

I'm too stunned to move. The saving grace is that I won't have much time to fret—we have to be packed and ready to leave by eight o'clock tomorrow morning.

Chapter Nine

# No Turning Back

*Wednesday, September 7*

Despite a sleepless night, the morning comes too quickly. Eight o'clock sharp we are packed, breakfasted, in the lobby, and ready to meet our trekking guide. In a white T-shirt, red baseball cap, and red silky athletic shorts, he's easy to spot among the uniformed resort staff and well-groomed guests.

With a wide smile that matches his broad body, and dark eyes that dance, he greets us. "I'm Gyanu, your guide."

I check out the bulging muscles on this man who stands no taller than I do at five-feet-three and think there's a good chance he could carry a broken body down the mountain if need be.

The hostess walks with us to the driveway at the resort entrance. She says, "I have never hiked in the Himalayas. It is my dream to become a guide. You will have a wonderful time." We smile and thank her. She asks, "Who is the travel agent?"

Joel tells her about Nanda Kulu. He adds, "It's Nanda's dream to train women to be guides."

As Joel and the hostess chat, I see her eyes shift away from Joel and go cold. I follow her stare and see our guide and another man push a white car towards us from across the parking lot. A third man sits at the wheel. The hostess locks her eyes on mine, presses a business card into my hand, and says, "If you need help, any help, call me!"

I clutch the card and worry about the car breaking down. I dismiss the idea of insisting on a different car—the driver probably needs the income he receives from this job. I can't take it away from him.

The engine starts and the car coasts over to us. Gyanu stands near the rear bumper with a skinny man half-a-head shorter than he is. "This is Urba. He will be your porter."

I glance at our oversized duffle bag and bright-blue, soft-sided roll-about with "Hawaii" printed across the front. I picture Urba sinking to the ground under their weight. Everything that seemed so essential to bring instantly loses its importance. The *sub*-sub-compact car parked in front of us may force a decision about what to take or leave. I go through a mental list of what we could do without. Sneakers, jeans, long-sleeve tops, and jackets to change into at night may not be necessary. We could get by with two pairs of socks and underwear instead of five if I wash them at night and hang them out to dry.

While I race through my list of discards, Gyanu, who must have worked in a sardine cannery in some previous life, squeezes our bags and Urba's and his gear into a trunk that has a four-grocery-sack capacity. He slides into the passenger seat next to the driver leaving Joel and me to sit in the back shoulder-to-shoulder with Urba, our backpacks wedged behind our heads. I am so fixated on the condition of the car we will be in for seven hours that I give the driver no more than a cursory glance and miss his name. He remains invisible and nameless for the rest of the trip. I have other things to think about. What I read in a guidebook knifes through my mind—airplane rides to and from the Himalayas are risky because of frequent crashes; the only thing worse is taking the roads.

We leave the city and the noise of traffic behind. Joel takes pictures as we pass terraced rice paddies and villages shrouded in gray smog, later bathed in sunlight as we travel further along.

"Why don't you close your eyes and get some sleep. You look awful," Joel says to me.

"Thanks!" flashes through my mind; that's just what I need to hear to make me feel worse. I close my eyes and try to sleep. Gyanu startles me from time-to-time with what sounds like "Crystal" at first and then "Fistal" later. Each time he points to the top of a snow-covered mountain suspended above the clouds. The brightness of its double peaks exceeds the whiteness of the clouds.

Later I learn Gyanu was saying "Fishtail," the name of the mountain derived from the shape of its double summits. Sacred to the god Shiva, it is forbidden to climb.

Joel wakes me when we stop for a potty break and lunch at an open-air restaurant with several shaded tables and two long counters lined with pots of food—one counter for Chinese, the other for Nepali dishes. Joel has sworn off Nepali food—we have Imodium on hand for his troubled digestive system. We stay with Chinese food, mostly noodles and vegetables.

After lunch he says, "I'm going to the bathroom." He knows I have public-bathroom issues and an amazing capacity to avoid them so he adds, "You'd better go, too. We have a long ride ahead."

I heed his warning, take a deep breath, and prepare for whatever unsightliness and stench I might encounter. I open the door. No smell, no mess, no toilet bowl either—just a porcelain rim with a bottomless basin set into a hole in the ground. Straddle, watch your feet, watch your aim. The first time I encountered an in-the-ground toilet, was at a restaurant somewhere in the hills of Italy. I had to ask my cousin for a how-to lesson. That lesson just came in handy.

We head to the parking lot in time to see four strangers pushing our car to get it started. It's familiar to us now. As long as the car doesn't have to stop for anything, we'll be okay. The engine catches and we hop in. As we get closer to the mountains, the two-lane road becomes one-and-a-half lanes where monsoon rains have chiseled away the edges. Cars pass on curves that back home would have solid double-yellow lines and prominent "Do Not Pass" signs. Here, rapid beeps of the car horn that reflect no sense of urgency on the drivers' part—at least not on our driver's—are the only warning to oncoming cars. I wonder, but don't want to find out, what happens when cars coming from opposite directions pass on a curve at the same time. Do they even hear each other's horn?

We round a bend and see a woman and several men laying parallel cables across the road.

"What are they for?" I ask.

"Accident. Maybe a bus went into the river. Maybe they will pull it up." Gyanu replies.

I lean across Joel and peek past Urba seated by the right window and see that the river's way down the mountainside. I sink back into my seat afraid to look again.

Less than a mile away, a bus lies on its side at the edge of the road, its nose pointing down toward the river. A few yards beyond it, a truck lies on its side in the opposite lane. I fasten my eyes to the asphalt ahead and shoot mental Spider-Man web-threads to hold our car on track. Joel is silent. He hasn't blinked for the last half-hour. He still has color in his face, so I guess he's okay.

Further along piles of dirt mark the start and end of road damage that exceeds the normal half-a-lane washout. A quick jerk of the wheel and we fly past it. It's a good thing it's daylight. I know how hard it is to see dirt piles in the dark—I once collided with one when I went for an early morning run.

By the time we arrive in Pokhara, the third largest city in Nepal, I am numb from seven hours of winding, beeping, and passing. We'll spend the night here before the start of our trek in the morning. We pull up to Hotel Gurkha Haven, a two-story orange and gray brick building with white balconies.

"You can see the high peaks from the roof, maybe," Gyanu tells us. "Eight of the ten highest peaks in the world are in Nepal." His face glows with pride; his smile spreads wider than ever.

A queen-size bed leaves just enough room to climb around our luggage; lumps in its mattress bulge through its dark-blue cover. An enclosed full bath is recessed into a corner of the room; an air conditioner that produces more noise than cool air rumbles non-stop. The room is basic, but I suspect it will look like the Ritz-Carlton when we return.

We drop our bags and head to the roof. Joel takes two steps at a time, checks every corner of the roof for views of mountains and finds that clouds obscure everything.

Disappointed, but optimistic, he says, "Maybe we'll see them tomorrow morning."

"You're starting to sound like Gyanu with the 'maybes.'"

"Maybe."

I give him a token punch on the arm and we head to our room to wash up and join Gyanu for a walk around Pokhara.

Unlike Kathmandu, sidewalks almost everywhere separate pedestrians from moving vehicles. But a new hazard surfaces—water buffalo roam the streets and sidewalks and leave traces of their wanderings. Thankful it's still daylight, I watch for buffalo splats and tap dance around them. By the time we finish dinner at a nearby restaurant, it's dark. I have to strain to see the variations in sidewalk shadings to avoid the patties in unlighted areas. Much of the time I follow immediately behind Gyanu mimicking his steps, slides, and hops. There is no time for conversation between Joel and me except for Joel's utterance, "Flashlights next time!"

It doesn't take long to see why Pokhara is a favorite place for trekkers to load up on gear—it's inexpensive and can be sold back at the end of a trek. At night the tourist area glows with colored lights from restaurants and hundreds of open stalls that line the streets. Each stall, no larger than a double garage, packs enough merchandise to fill a good-sized boutique in the U.S. I slip behind a curtain in one shop, try on North Face hiking tops and buy two at $8.50 each instead of the thirty dollars I would pay at home. Unlike my cotton-knit tops, one of which is plastered to me from Nepal's heat and humidity, the new tops should wick away the sweat. Tomorrow will be the first test of the theory.

I turn to Gyanu and ask more than say, "I read somewhere that we should buy leech oil."

Gyanu replies, "You don't need it. It's stinky. You will not like it." A few feet away, he stops at a street vendor and buys a small drawstring bag of something. I'm curious about what's in it, but I don't ask and he doesn't tell.

Gyanu walks us back to the hotel and says, "We will meet at 7:00 and go to Nayapul. Then we trek."

"How far away is Nayapul from here?" Joel asks.

"Maybe one-and-a-half hours."

"Are the roads better or the same as the ones today?" I ask, fingers crossed behind my back.

"Maybe not so good."

The warm-up for the trek is working: my fear of trekking takes a backseat to being a passenger in a car.

Chapter Ten

# MUD, RICE, AND RAIN

## (Nayapul to Hile)

*Thursday, September 8—Trek Day 1*

"Would you like to borrow sleeping bags?" the innkeeper asks as we are loading up promptly at 7 a.m.

My eyes shift to Gyanu who says, "Maybe sometimes you do not want to sleep on the bed."

We add two sleeping bags to Urba's load, squeeze into the car, and head to Nayapul, the starting point for our trek. Gyanu's description of the road as "maybe-not-so-good" turns out to be an understatement. I sit behind him in the car and hope that whatever gods watch over him will watch over me as well.

We arrive in Nayapul a little before 9:00 a.m. The driver lets us out on a rocky dirt road lined on one side with open-front shacks that sell soft drinks, snacks, and cigarettes. A palpable undercurrent of tension drifts through the drop-off area no larger than a bus stop; a dense morning fog makes for an eerie beginning. After the driver unloads our bags, he says good-bye, and drives off. Another car pulls up and four young men bound out, sling packs on their shoulders, and, in a flash, disappear from sight while we remain looking around and fussing with our stuff.

"In season lots of cars would be here," Gyanu says.

"When does the season begin?" Joel asks.

"In two weeks."

Lucky us, shoots through my mind; the taste of sarcasm coats each word. Had we come to Nepal two weeks later, we wouldn't have been able to arrange a trek on the spur of the moment. All the guides would have been booked and I would be back at the resort taking short hikes around Kathmandu by day and sauna-ing by night.

Urba ties our bags together and slides them onto his back. A wide, cloth band worn across his forehead and strapped to the load helps distribute the weight. Gyanu, anxious to get started, signals for us to follow. I take a deep breath and do what I always do when I'm afraid but have no choice other than to continue—I lock my fear deep inside, ignore it, and move on.

Gyanu, out ahead of us, clears our way through two checkpoints. We catch up with him at the second Tims Check Post, where he chats with the official standing behind the counter in the garage-like office.

With our trekking permits stamped for approval, we are officially on our way. We pass horses the size of donkeys loaded with goods to bring up the mountain, shops with wares hung out on display, motorcycles, and small trucks that replenish the shops' supplies. Soon we cross a bridge to where the trail begins.

Urba, our porter, loading up in Nayapul.

Here I am walking through the town. Gyanu walks ahead in
the middle of the road.

So far so good, but the piece-of-cake walk doesn't last long. A mud slide blocks the path.

With a shrug, Gyanu says, "People cut wood to keep warm in winter. They don't leave any trees. When the monsoons come, the mudslides come. We go up there." He points toward a mudslide as tall as a six story building dotted with trekkers and locals making their way up or down. My heart sinks into my feet; I don't do slippery well.

Three-steps-up and two-slides-back repeat in rapid succession as I attack the slimy rubble coated with black, clay-laden mud. My deep-grooved hiking boots do no better than plastic glides used to move heavy furniture across carpet. If I didn't have my walking stick to dig into the sludge, there would be no forward progress. I send out a plaintive cry to summon Gyanu, who is almost half-way to the top. He returns and extends his hand. I seize it with the desperation of a drowning person and maintain the death grip as he drags me to the top of the slide.

He leaves me anchored to a fallen tree trunk and heads part-way down to help an elderly Nepali woman with the climb. Only then do I dare to look for Joel. He is half-way up negotiating the slick incline on his own. When I turn back, I see that somehow Gyanu is ahead of me again. I have no choice but to move on. I slip-slop across the top of the half-moon path and then gasp as I survey the path down. The six stories grow to eight in my mind. I lock my eyes on the mud slope, freeze my brain to shut out the "Oh no!" it blasts, and begin my skid downward. With knees shaking, walking stick wobbling, and my body engaged in a jerking dance, I murmur to myself, "I'm so screwed. I'm so screwed."

When I reach the bottom I ask Gyanu, "Will we have to cross this on the return?"

I hold my breath until he answers, "No." That's all I want to know for now.

I regain my equilibrium, and continue on. Urba, who in flip-flops had cleared the mudslide well before us, sits on the side of the dirt road waiting. The crowd of people on the mudslide disperses along the trail leaving Joel and me to trek alone with our guide and porter. By eleven o'clock we are away from Nayapul and well along the path that will lead us to Poon Hill in a couple of days.

Urba our porter (left) and Gyanu our guide taking a break.

We amble along slowly gaining altitude. We'll reach five-thousand feet by end of day. This is no problem for Joel and me; we have spent the summer walking along roads like this and hiking in the Southern Rockies at close to ten thousand feet.

Twists and turns in the inclined path obscure our view of what lies ahead. Gyanu, like a machine, moves steadily on unless we call to him to stop so we can look around.

From a height I barely knew we had gained, Joel and I gaze at the light green color of the terraced rice paddies, so different from the barren, stone-covered surfaces we had expected. The dark green of the leafy trees that surround the paddies make their bright color even more striking. Joel with his camera and I with my eyes follow the ridges of rounded mountains. Their steep slopes crisscross in the fog-filled valleys between them.

Thunderous waterfalls plummet from mountaintops. Foamy white streams swollen from monsoon rains cut through boulders and across our path; their sound is as fascinating and frightening as the Atlantic Ocean's in a winter storm. Sturdy, wood-plank bridges hung from cables sway as they span the waters. Five-foot high nets of rope strung along the bridges' sides remove any fear of falling.

I'm thankful it's not logs, stones, and prayers that I have to rely on to get across.

I'm busy chatting and not paying attention when Joel grabs my collar and yanks me back. A family of water buffalo approaches. Their slow, uninterrupted movement makes it clear there is an understood stop sign for us. They cut in front, head for the pond on our left, dip and then recline in the water indifferent to our picture-taking. I wish I could join them. It's not even mid-day and I'm drenched from the humidity and unobstructed sunlight that burned away the fog a long time ago. My new hiking shirt may wick sweat away, but, I swear, it wicks it straight to the top of my head and soaks the hair buried under my baseball cap. Joel still looks cool—I envy how well he tolerates heat.

Water buffalo soaking in a pond.

Lines of pack horses and Nepali men and women carrying goods from Nayapul pass us now and then. I carry only my walking stick and water in the CamelBak hung from my shoulders; that's enough weight for me to bear.

"In tourist season, there would be people walking up and down the trail," Gyanu volunteers. I picture streams of trekkers and think how lucky we are—no tourists, no heads in the way of pictures, and no worry that I'm going too slow for the people behind me.

Pack horses alongside Joel (left) and Gyanu (right).

We break for lunch at a teahouse, a two or three room wooden house that has an outdoor terrace where trekkers can sit, refuel, and refresh. I order vegetarian dal bhat—lentil soup served with steamed rice. Joel orders a bland noodle dish for his challenged stomach. We pick a table to sit at; Gyanu and Urba disappear from sight. After we talk for a while, I notice a woman amble out of the house with a pot in her hand. She walks across the road to a spigot protruding from a four-foot high stone wall built into the mountain. She turns the water on and tosses noodles under it several times. A couple of minutes later, she serves our food. I don't dare let Joel know his *safe* food has just been bathed in untreated mountain water. I'll tell him to stick to rice or lentils next time.

After the lunch break, the climb becomes steeper. The path turns into three-foot-wide steps made of stacked stones, each four- to eight-inches high. These paths connect occasional teahouses and lodges.

I grew up climbing steps. My family's apartment was on the seventh floor of low-income projects in Brooklyn, New York. Whenever I could, I took the stairs instead of the elevator that smelled like a toilet. I never dreamed the stair-climbing would prepare me for a trek in the Himalayas—my dreams never stretched that far.

The further up we go, the more dramatic the silent beauty of the terraced rice fields becomes. The paddies we see now will, in dryer seasons, become fields of soy and corn.

"People grow most of the food they eat. What they cannot grow or make, they order from Nayapul," Gyanu tells us as we gaze at the landscape.

"How do they place orders?" I ask.

"They have telephones."

Terraced rice fields.

The rest of the afternoon we continue to climb dry and then muddy steps; my feet are set on automatic. Joel tugs at my CamelBak to signal me to stop.

"What?"

"Listen."

The muted clang of bells attached to the necks of packhorses echoes around us. The haunting, melodic sound matches the slow, side-to-side sway of the horses as they pick their way along trails.

Joel listens to their sound; I watch my feet. The lines of packhorses that precede us choose the best places to step. They leave droppings as evidence to prove it.

I marvel at how Nepali women traverse the terrain with graceful ease in flip-flops. Even elderly women have no trouble flip-flopping up or down the mountain on steps made slippery by mud and matter. Maybe they're not really old but just look that way, worn from having to climb rocky stairs each day.

Urba climbing steps between villages.

Up ahead we see a water buffalo move onto the path; his body, set on a diagonal, leaves no room to pass. Gyanu and Urba are well on the other side of the obstruction, oblivious to our dilemma.

Ever polite, I say, "Excuse me." The buffalo, with an annoyed look in his eye, rears his rear right leg and gives it a couple of thrusts. There is no way I'm going to push him aside.

"Now what?"

Joel has no reply. The quiet man studies the situation; his impatient partner says, "BEEP, BEEP!" That does the trick. The buffalo must be a fan of New York City movies with honking cabbies. He moves out of the way without hesitation and we continue on bathed in heat and humidity. I make a mental note to tell anyone who considers a trek in the Himalayas to do hours of Stair-Master, spend time in the Rockies to get used to the altitude, and have a desire to experience what Houston would feel like in the middle of summer without air conditioning.

Toward the end of the six-hour hike, drenching rain greets us. The cool drops feel good against my hot, tired body. I'm already soaked from the inside out; it doesn't matter if I get soaked from the outside in.

By 5:00 p.m. we arrive at the Annapurna Guest House in Hile. I drip past the front desk and wooden dining tables and head for the porch where I plop down on a chair and ask for a cup of jasmine tea. I don't feel human again until I warm my hands on the glass mug and inhale the steamy scent rising from it. After a few sips I take in the view of fog shrouded mountains. The bright yellow ears of corn that hang to dry from the second story balcony punctuate the cheerfulness of the white teahouse trimmed with peacock-blue. This is not bad! I had thought we would be sharing a room with others in a dimly lit wooden shack with an outhouse or, worse yet, a hole in the floor in the corner of the room to use as a toilet.

Hile: Annapurna Guest House.

The owner of the guest house shows us to our room on the second floor that opens onto the balcony with the hanging corn. Left of our door is a sink to share with other guests and perpendicular to it a door behind which is a Nepali style toilet. There is a shower, but we don't have towels and the guest house doesn't provide any. The owner gives us a key to lock the padlock on the door when we leave the room.

Wood-trimmed windows with views of the mountains let abundant light into the room. Two twin-size beds, pushed against opposite walls, have just enough room between them for a small table. Joel and I bump heads as we bend to peel off our wet clothes. The mattresses look like stone slabs, but feel like memory-foam.

Annapurna Guest House bedroom.

Joel in the dining room.

It's not even six o'clock and Joel snoozes away. I wash our socks and underwear, hang them outside to dry on a line under the eaves along with our hats and hiking clothes, and then wake Joel to go downstairs to dinner. The owner fusses over us and scurries about to prepare our meal—dal bhat. There appear to be no other guests.

Gyanu stops by to chat and make sure we have gotten dinner. I ask him how far we had hiked.

"Nobody knows. Every time they measure, it is different."

He tells us to get some rest and adds, "Tomorrow is a long day."

"How long?" I ask.

He smiles but does not answer.

Chapter Eleven

# Is It Over Yet?

(Hile to Ghorepani)

*Friday, September 9—Trek Day 2*

"Leeches? No leeches. Only when it rains a lot. Monsoon almost finished. Maybe it rains a little." Gyanu's words rattled through my mind as I lay in bed last night and listened to the unrelenting rain splash against the window next to my bed.

We wake to a foggy morning. Today we will climb over 4,000 feet to a height of 9,240—almost as high as our summer home in the Southern Rockies at 9,500 feet. There's a cold-water shower two doors down from our room, but the absence of towels gives us an excuse to stay in bed an extra half-hour.

Still groggy from a sleep made restless by the rains, I pluck our hiking clothes from the sheltered clothesline and find they are as wet as they were last night when I hung them out to dry. Joel, half asleep, packs the wet underwear and hiking tops into a corner of our duffle bag, but leaves out our hiking pants and hats.

"They'll have to dry on us," he says as he forces a foot into his pant leg and snaps a soggy baseball cap onto his head. We have to conserve on hiking pants; we have only one other pair for the five days. I follow suit, donning my clammy clothes, thankful the air is warm.

With our bags stacked outside the door for Urba to retrieve, we head down to breakfast.

A young man sits on a stool near the front desk, "May I show you jewelry I make?" His serious expression, soft voice, and dark eyes stop just short of pleading.

"I'm sorry. We didn't bring enough money with us to buy anything," Joel says with compassion written across his face. Tips for drivers and having to pay cash for meals have left us short.

"My family is from Tibet. They show me how to make beautiful jewelry."

I don't want to hurt his feelings, waste his time, or raise his hopes so I say, "If you would like, you can show us the jewelry, but I'm afraid we cannot buy any."

The young man doesn't ask again; he disappears without a word. My heart sinks further.


Eight o'clock sharp, Gyanu appears at the entry. He's wearing the same red shorts and white T-shirt he had on yesterday, but his hair is spikey wet, probably drip-drying from a towel-less shower.

Joel jokes with Gyanu about our wet clothes and then turns to Urba and says, "Sorry. We wrung the clothes out, but you will still have an extra pound of water to carry."

Urba doesn't understand a word Joel says, but smiles anyway. Gyanu translates and then says to us "If you hang them on your backpack, they will dry."

We dig the wet clothes out of our bag and secure them to our packs. Joel looks especially cute with his Jockeys hung in full view. My underwear is discretely tucked next to my hiking top. Feeling as if we look more like experienced trekkers, we head out to Ghorepani.

Heading to Ghorepani with laundry draped on my CamelBak to dry. It's the start of day two of the trek.

Our climb resumes on stone steps made slippery from last night's rains. Gyanu and Urba have climbed these steps, wet or dry, all their lives and negotiate them with ease. The slipperiness, added to watching for horse droppings, further slows my pace.

We encounter narrow streams created by the rains and cross them on wet stones that barely rise above the gently flowing water. Gyanu gives me a hand. Joel bounds from one stone to another as if he's on dry land. He taps me on the shoulder and says, "Listen."

In the near-silence that surrounds us, once again I hear the soft ring of bells on pack horses echo through the mountain; their wooden strikers create a muted, melodic sound like bells of ethereal cathedrals.

Streams and villages dot the landscape.

Distances between teahouses become greater, open views of rice fields become less frequent; bright green ferns and tangled, leafy shrubs close in on the trail. Waterfalls, the height and volume of which would qualify them to be national monuments in our country, are commonplace here. Instead of looking up at the falls as we did at the beginning of the trek, we are high enough now to look both up and down. Their roar is mesmerizing.

Gyanu waits as Joel takes pictures from the safety of a bridge and I stand next to him inhaling the cool freshness of the water-sprayed air. Gyanu's smile shows pride in our pleasure; but his body languages states we have a long way to go and have to move on.

Waterfall on the way to Ghorepani.

Partway up a particularly steep incline, I stop short to catch my breath where the steps make a sharp left turn. Joel, behind me, becomes aware of my abrupt pause too late. I sense a desperate movement and snap my head around in time to see him start to fall backwards over the edge of the rocky steps. His arms windmill as he tries to catch his balance; the weight of his backpack pulls him down. My hand shoots back, grabs the first part of him it catches—his crotch—and pulls him to safety.

"Leave something to grab for next time," he says between clenched teeth as his painful grimace subsides.

The sun breaks through, but not enough to counter the humidity. Two hours into the hike, last night's laundry is still wet; the clothes we have on are equally soggy. The mountainside gets steeper, the steps higher. Gyanu sets a pace I cannot sustain. I turn to Joel and say, "I have to stop," and with my last sizeable breath call to Gyanu to wait. He can't hear me; he wears earphones to listen to music on his iPod. Joel lends his booming voice to the effort. It's no use.

"He'll turn around eventually and see we're missing in action," I say with an air of resignation.

Gyanu is well out of sight, hidden by twists and turns in the path ahead. When we catch up to him, we find him sitting on a stone wall talking with some of the locals. I think he knows half the people on the mountain and makes these treks so he can visit with them.

He greets us with a warm smile and then leads us further along the trail to the stone patio of a teahouse. Two brown-skinned girls with thick, dark hair tied back from their softly-rounded faces, sit on their heels with graceful ease as they scrub pots and pans under water from a hose. With smiles as big as Gyanu's, they greet him and chat while Joel and I find a place to relax nearby.

From my seat on a low stone wall, I watch the fluid movements of the girls. An invisible but palpable stream of joy connects Gyanu with them. Their youth and quiet happiness convert the damp grayness of the day into warmth and comfort. I want to take a picture to hold onto what I see and later remember the peace I feel. My hand itches for my camera so I can snap away as I have done so many times with unsuspecting subjects. In this setting, doing so feels wrong. But if I ask permission, I fear their naturalness may become stiff and formal, the mood lost. I tuck the camera by my side, smother my impetuousness, and approach Gyanu.

"Would it be all right if I take a picture of the girls?"

He translates my request and they reply with a giggle, "Just take our faces, not our bodies." They motion that they don't want pot-washing to show in the picture. I take their faces, bodies, pots, and pans and tell them that even the pot-washing is beautiful to me.

Nepali girls washing pots and pans at a teahouse
along the way.

Too few minutes of rest and we're back to stair-stepping up the mountain. Gyanu pulls out his iPod and I say to him, "Do you think you could listen to the iPod with just one earplug instead of two?" He smiles, takes the earphones off, and puts the iPod away. Now he walks ahead of us and talks with Urba. I fall only once—nothing much. I slip, land on rocks, and bounce back up. No damage. Gyanu, oblivious to the fall, continues with an unbroken pace. Anger at his lack of attention and a fear of losing track of him replace my dread of falling. The steady steps of Joel walking behind me ward off any possibility of panic.

Approaching a village along the way to Ghorepani.

By the time we stop for lunch at one o'clock, we have done the equivalent of five hours of Stair-Master. I send a mental message to my thighs and buttocks to forget the morning ever happened. They ignore me. For once, Joel looks as worn as I feel. I make a weak attempt at conversation and suggest we create a slide show to distribute electronically to friends who want to hear about our trek. He replies, "I'm not sure I want to tell anyone about this." I mull this over for a minute; somehow it eases my complaining mind.

At the end of the hour, we drag our tortured bodies back on the trail. Gyanu, with his usual boyish smile and exuberance, says the steps are less steep; my legs say otherwise. Any hope for the steps to dry is vanquished by intermittent rain. We pull our rain jackets out of Joel's backpack, put our cameras in, and then do the reverse each time the rain stops and starts. The rain forest surrounding the rice fields gets closer, closes in on us in patches, and finally immerses us in its dark wetness. The drenching rain continues to pour down through the narrow opening in the canopy that the trail creates.

Gyanu says, "There are monkeys, musk deer, tigers, and wild cats in there. You not see them, because they not coming near the trail. They are afraid of people."

It's getting dark. I'm wet. I'm cold. I don't care about big cats, monkeys, and musk whatever-they-are. I just keep walking.

Joel calls to Gyanu and points to an inch-long, black thing no wider than a few strands of hair that slithers along his left hand. It looks and moves like a dark cousin to an inchworm. With speed and precision, Gyanu snatches the leech from Joel's skin. A few steps late Joel summons Gyanu again.

Gyanu says to Joel, "Maybe you rub against leaves."

We see leeches on the shrubs. Their cantilevered bodies stretch beyond the edge of a leaf poised to latch onto an unsuspecting dinner that passes by. One suck and they can expand up to ten times their size and won't have to feast for a month.

A few leeches later, I spot where they're coming from. They live in the wet, leaf-matted ground on which we are tramping. The vibrations from Gyanu's and my footsteps announce a blood source to them just in time for the leeches to find Joel who walks third in line. They're crawling up his walking stick. Extracting them has to be done carefully so they don't regurgitate into your bloodstream and possibly cause an infection. After a while, Joel becomes adept at leech removal. With speed that equals Gyanu's, he grabs the bulging head and as much of the body as he can between two fingers and yanks it off his skin.

He turns to me and says "The trick is to get it before it starts feeding."

You don't feel leeches, but their black, slithering bodies show up nicely against light clothes and skin. Gyanu checks my limbs, but doesn't see any creepy crawlers. If they latch onto me as I trudge further along, I don't notice; I'm preoccupied with planting my walking stick ahead of me to pull myself up the next six- to eight-inch high step. The chilling rain lacks the cooling comfort it had in the heat of the day. I'm on the verge of using age as an excuse to beg Gyanu to drag me up or slow down when I recall the story he told last night.

He had a client who contacted him each year to arrange a private trek. The client suffered from Parkinson's disease; his tremors were controlled by medication. The man had clearance from his doctor to trek, carried plenty of medicine with him, had great stamina, walked with gusto, and hiked faster than Gyanu.

"How old was he," I asked.

"Sixty-seven."

Exactly my age. That eliminated age-related, sympathy-getting excuses I had stored for use on the trek.

Sorrow replaced his exuberance as Gyanu told us, "One morning we start to hike. He collapsed. I carried him to the medic station, but it was too late. He was dead."

I felt the eager, up-beat expression on my face droop into sadness. Joel remained silent. I managed an "Oh."


By 5:15 p.m. my legs, back, and buttocks tell my feet they are not going any further. The steps had steadily increased in height as we climbed higher throughout the day. It takes a few minutes for my mind to override my body's command and set my feet in motion again. Guesthouses, something we haven't seen for a couple of hours, appear up ahead. We pass each lodge without stopping. A while later I think I see Nirvana—a three-story lodge painted white, with a blue roof, and a big welcome sign hung from a balcony.

"Is that our lodge?" I feel myself light up for the first time since this morning.

"No. It's the one up there."

My eyes trace a line from Gyanu's shoulder to his pointing finger and up the mountainside.

I chuckle, "You're joking."

He shakes his head "No."

"Yes, you are!"

"No. That is where we stay."

Another half a mountain to scale, or so it seems to my step-weary body.

"Can we warm up and get dry there?" Joel asks. He looks as wet and miserable as I feel.

"Maybe. I will ask the owner to heat some space."

After eight and a half hours of hiking, what looms ahead is a half-hour climb up the steepest part of the mountain so far. Each step is eighteen to twenty-four inches high. I have to lift my knees halfway to my chest to climb them. Partway up, Gyanu reaches for my hand and drags me the remaining distance to Hotel Snow Land, our home for the night. Although I don't have the energy to look back for Joel, I know he's walking behind me as he promised he would. The pounding rain all but smothers the sound of his labored footsteps. He doesn't speak a word.

We step out of the dark, wet night into the warmly lighted entry of the lodge. A fire burns under a large hot water tank in the middle of the room. Horizontal two-by-fours spaced two feet apart form a cage around the tank. Three Japanese trekkers, two women and a man, all in their twenties, sit on benches close to the heat; their clothes hang on the boards to dry. They look rested and their smiles say they are eager to converse. It takes a few minutes for us to respond. Joe nods hello. I smile. We sit with our backs to the fire, and relish the warmth. We place our wet boots as close to the fire as we dare and drape our soggy socks on the boards.

"The heat feels good," Joel says.

"Yes," They respond in chorus, stretching "yes" into two syllables.

"Have you been here a while?" I ask.

"Yes. We arrived two hours ago," answers one of the women. "Don't feel bad. Last night we were like you. We were the last to arrive."

I don't feel bad; I just feel happy that I *did* arrive.

"Are you friends or cousins?" They look too different from each other and too close in age to ask if they are siblings.

They laugh and shake their heads, "No."

The young man answers, "We met online." He points to the girl nearest me and says, "She sent a message on the Internet to ask if anyone wanted to trek." He pauses and then continues, "We met each other for the first time when we went to Tokyo to plan the trip."

The girl who initiated the trek says, "We are doing twelve-day trek to ABC (Annapurna Base Camp). Are you?"

"No, just the five-day to Poon Hill."

She turns away from her companions and says to me, "I'm afraid! I do not want to go to ABC."

My eyes search hers, but all I can manage to say is, "Don't worry. You'll be fine," and hope she believes me.

Gyanu suggests we place our orders for dinner. Custom or rule, every lodge/guesthouse/teahouse must have the same menu, but each interprets the recipes differently. As a result, we never know what we will get. We order meatless meals: lentils for me noodles for Joel, and let the innkeeper know we would like to change into dry clothes before dinner.

We climb two flights of uneven steps holding on to loose bannisters and walk down a barely lighted, narrow corridor made darker by its wood-panel walls. We unlock the padlock on the door, turn on the light, and find we have a luxury suite by trekkers' standards. The bedroom has twin beds with a window between them. On the other side of the room, a door opens to a private bathroom. It has a European style toilet—the first we have seen since leaving Pokhara. Pipes, mounted on a painted, dark blue wall, lead to a shower head. Hand written in broad strokes of white paint above round knobs are the words "Hot" and "Cold." Folded towels lie on top of the toilet tank next to the sink.

We save the hot water shower for later, change into dry clothes, and take the wet ones from yesterday and today downstairs to hang by the water heater.

Joel tries to pay for dinner with American dollars. The woman behind the desk examines the money, shakes her head, straightens her back, and pushes the money away.

Gyanu translates, "The money is no good. It has a crease. The bank will not take it."

We have to borrow Nepali money from Gyanu, which can be creased or otherwise mutilated, to pay the bill.

Before saying goodnight, Gyanu says to us, "Tomorrow maybe we climb Poon Hill. If there are no clouds we can see high peaks. I knock on your door at 4:15. We have to leave at 4:30 to see the sunrise. If there are clouds, I won't knock. You can sleep."

Joel and I shower and lay out our clothes for the next day so we can dress in fifteen minutes. We don't have winter jackets; we have to layer. Joel offers a spare undershirt; I take it and add a cotton turtleneck, my Old Navy polyester vest, and an REI fleece jacket to tomorrow's pile. Joel's stack looks a lot like mine.

I lie in bed, stare out the window, and pray for clouds. I don't care that the climb to Poon Hill at sunrise is the highlight of the trek; my body and mind need a rest.

I compose a postcard in my head to send to family and friends, "Wish you were here . . . instead of me." But if I write that, I lose my bragging rights. I doze off still waiting for clouds to darken the moonlit sky.

## Chapter Twelve
# UPS AND DOWNS
### (Poon Hill to Tadapani)

*Saturday, September 10—Trek Day 3*

I felt guilty for praying for clouds last night. I knew the morning sunrise might be our only chance to see the tall Annapurna peaks and that Joel would be disappointed if we missed them, but I prayed anyway. Little did I know Joel was praying as hard as I was for the same thing. Gyanu, on the other hand, must have prayed for clear skies and his prayers proved more powerful than ours.

It's 4 a.m. I awake to the sound of a knock on the door. I call, "Okay," jump out of bed, and scramble for my clothes. Joel, shivering alongside me, hustles into his.

"It's friggin' cold in here," he mutters as he wobbles on one foot and then the other, pulling on his hiking pants.

At 4:15, Gyanu knocks on the door; his quizzical expression registers surprise that we are dressed and ready to go. The questioning look in his eyes confuses me at first and then I realize that the walls of the guest house provide as effective a sound barrier as a shower curtain—the 4:00 knock must have been on someone else's door.

With vests and jackets layered over our clothes and headlamps strapped to our foreheads, we chase after Gyanu as he runs down the corridor to the stairs. We see the young Japanese man we met last night bolt out the front door just ahead of us and disappear into the darkness.

Within a few strides we leave the open area and enter a shrub-lined path that is just shy of the width of my body. The moonlight doesn't penetrate the foliage; all I can see is the spot in front of me illuminated by my headlamp. I aim my light at Gyanu's heels and tear past the twigs that tug at my jacket.

And then come the stone steps.

Gyanu doesn't wait for a request. He grabs my hand and pulls me up the steps, each one eighteen to twenty-four inches high. My knees fire like pistons as they rise to my chest and then push down in an unbroken rhythm. We move at Gyanu's speed, not mine. Joel's heavy breathing answers my own.

We pause on a three-foot wide, flat area and look down at hills and an occasional house silhouetted in moonlight.

With an urgency I have not heard before, Gyanu says, "Look! The sun is coming up. We must hurry."

I didn't know we weren't hurrying.

Forty-five minutes of high-stepping up more than 1,300 feet to an altitude of 10,600 and we emerge from the path onto the flat, cold, wind-swept top of Poon Hill just as the sun begins to creep over the horizon. The site before me takes away what little breath I have left. Peaks, pure white in their snow-covered brightness, form an unbroken chain that wraps half-way around a three hundred sixty degree vista. Set against the semi-darkness of early sunrise, the summits glow in the thin, mountain air. They dominate horizontal layers of striated clouds that cut across all but the highest peaks and lend a soft palette of contrast.

I rush to the far end of the open expanse, half the size of a football field, to get as close to the miles-away peaks as I can. Silent and majestic, the summits seem to sunbathe in the crisp air, indifferent to their grandeur. Cocooned in fascination, I gaze left-to-right in a sweeping arc and back again marveling at the irregular forms and their reflected brilliance. I don't notice the wind or the cold any longer. I feel like nothing more than a curious piece of inconsequential matter, but an extraordinarily happy one at that.

Annapurna's high peaks from the top of Poon Hill. Lesser mountains and valleys lie between where I stand and the peaks.

Fishtail (Machhapuchhre) at 23,000 feet. Annapurna I, the highest peak at 26,500 feet (not shown here), is also visible from Poon Hill.

Other tourists—fifty or more—mostly young Asian and Anglo men and women pose for pictures. I don't know where so many trekkers came from; I didn't see them on the trails. It doesn't matter. They become invisible to me as I stare at the mountains trying to take in everything I can before the sunlight brightens, the peaks fade, and more clouds eclipse the view.

Joel says, "Stay where you are," and snaps a picture, one of many he takes to preserve this moment. A willing tourist takes a picture of Joel and me standing together and then I retrieve my camera, the backup camera, and start to take photos, too; I want to remember Poon Hill as I see it.

As the sun continues to rise, the contrast between bright and dark lessons. My body awakens to the cold with a shudder. Joel suggests we get something hot to drink. That's when I first notice the shack in which a young Nepali man stands with steaming pots of water, a big smile, and a knitted cap with flaps that drape over his ears. He, with a partner, had carried gallons of water up the same steps we climbed (bless him!) and heated it before any of us arrived.

The young man charges three times the normal price, but it's worth it. The mug of hot, fragrant tea feels good against my cold-reddened hands and even better as it slides into my body.

Joel calls Gyanu over and treats him to a cup of coffee; Urba, our porter, declines.

While we sip our hot drinks, Gyanu shares a bit of history. "Poon is my caste. A Poon guy saw such a beautiful view from the hill. He named the hill for his caste. Poon Hill."

Joel and Gyanu at the portable teahouse at the top of Poon Hill.

Joel and I at the top of Poon Hill.

By 6 a.m. the clouds hide the peaks, it's light out, and we head back to the hotel for a breakfast of eggs and flat bread. A sense of triumph and exhilaration from the early morning climb equals, but does not trump, the image of brilliant peaks that glides across my mind.

The young Japanese girl who organized the twelve-day trek to the Annapurna Base Camp sits alone.

"Did you see the peaks?" I ask.

"No."

"Why?"

"I wanted to sleep."

My heart sinks, but I don't say anything—I had been willing to miss Poon Hill, too.

After breakfast we gather our things and leave the hotel in Ghorepani. I check my watch and see it's only 9:30, the time I might be just getting out of bed back home.

We head for Tadapani hiking through a mixture of rain forests and open areas. We soak up every bit of sunshine we can in the periods between drenchings. Rest stops made of stacked stone that look like five-foot tall Mayan ruins appear just when we become desperate for a break. German tourists trekking the Himalayas from the opposite direction join us at one. From our resting point we watch a man galloping towards us. He bounds off rocks that I so carefully negotiate. He interrupts his run long enough to say he is trekking on his own, running between stops at guest houses. What could I possibly say to this thirtyish American, long and lean, who wears a T-shirt, running shorts, and running shoes; all he carries is a wallet and a change of underwear. Booted up, portered, and guided, I feel a bit overdone.

"Next time, we'll travel lighter," Joel says into my ear.

"Next time, we'll bring more dry clothes," is what I think but don't say.

The Germans stand around getting lazy with us until one girl lets out a screech.

"Leeches!" She jumps off the rest stop. We all scramble to grab our things and split in different directions.

Urba, Gyanu, and Joel at a rest area along the trail.

By two-thirty, five hours into our hike from Ghorepani through gusting winds and a downpour, we approach a teahouse for lunch. Mini boulders hold down its tin roof; wind tears at its edges. We're grateful the dining room is enclosed. We hang our jackets on separate wall hooks and see from puddles beneath them that at least two other hikers have been here before us. Joel chooses a dry bench to sit on at one of the dozen long dining tables. In season, the room fills with trekkers; but for now, we are the only guests.

Gyanu, as usual, disappears into the kitchen to spend time with the owner. He reappears after a while to make sure we have been served and have everything we need and then disappears again. Urba, ever silent, is nowhere to be seen. The staff is pleasant and attentive, but, as in other places we have been, doesn't socialize with us. I don't know whether it is out of respect for our privacy or desire for their own.

The rain stops. It re-starts an hour later, just as we're about to leave.

A few steps from the teahouse and we're back in the rain forest. A dense canopy darkens the path, but doesn't block the steady splash of rain. Bright green ferns crowd the edges of the trail. Broad and narrow-leafed plants drape a living wall around us. Glimmering leaves grow under, on top of, and through each other making it hard to tell where one plant ends and the other begins. I spot an occasional yellow or red flower and suspect that most flowers have drowned in the monsoon. We hike mostly down, but sometimes up, slick steps.

Hiking through the rain forest between Ghorepani and
Tadapani during a break in the rain.

For two-and-a-half hours I sidestep down glistening
rocks coated with the equivalent of black ice. The yellow
stones, smooth or grooved, are the worst. The metallic
sound of my walking stick as it strikes rock after rock
pierces the steady patter of rain and the near-silence of the
forest around us.

Gyanu becomes my second walking stick—much
better than the metal one I carry. He uses two different
hand grips to announce treacherous footing. When he holds
just my fingers as if we are dancing a minuet, the hazard is

tolerable. A full handshake means trouble. I brace myself each time he employs it knowing what's about to happen. One foot slips out, and then the other. My body does a zombie jerk back and forth. This repeats for the next few steps until I re-establish my balance. The only thing that keeps me from slamming my tailbone onto the rocks is Gyanu's grip. I almost take him out a couple of times.

My dark sunglasses, coupled with the hand-holding, create a false picture. I look as if I'm a blind person being led down the mountain and doing an admirable job instead of a wimp holding on for dear life.

I know the sunglasses add a hazard in the dim, forest light but I'm afraid to free a hand for even a moment to remove them. I say several *Hail Marys*, a prayer I haven't said in fifty-years, and think of saying the whole rosary, but that would take too much concentration. I vow I will construct hiking boots with retractable suction cups if I ever decide to trek in monsoon season again.

Slipping and sliding down slopes doesn't seem to bother Joel as he follows two stone-steps behind me. He catches his balance, stops to take pictures, slips some more, and moves on.

"Louise, you have to see this."

"I can't. I'll break my neck if I turn around."

My eyes look past my trembling knees to the next step. I don't dare look elsewhere. I'm startled by a kick in the butt that makes me shift to a wide stance. I stiffen to support myself and the landslide that is Joel.

"What was that for?" I ask.

"I'm sorry. It was an accident." Amazement sparkles in Joel's eyes as he picks himself up and brushes himself off.

"I didn't know I could kick so high!"

The image of his chorus line kick to my butt makes me laugh out loud. It plays over and over in my mind, takes the place of the *Hail Marys*, and lightens the rest of the day's hike.

After seven-and-a-half hours of hiking, added to the hour-and-a-half it took to hike up and then down Poon Hill, we arrive in Tadapani. Like the night before, the guest house Gyanu has selected is the furthest up the steep hill before us. It's lovely, large, and clean—it's also closed. The innkeeper tells us the bathrooms are not working; she is not allowed to have guests. I'm tempted to say I would be happy to use an outhouse if I could stay here, but sense it's useless to ask.

Gyanu uses his cell phone to call his friend who owns a guest house part-way down the hill—BUT it's not open yet for the season. A call to another place secures rooms at the bottom of the hill we just climbed. The innkeeper at the broken-bathroom inn suggests a shortcut using a dirt path she says is easier than the steps.

Down through the trees and shrubs along a leaf-matted path we march. Gyanu bats leeches off his shoes, legs, and arms. I do the same. Joel, the leech magnet, plucks away. The steep, slippery steps I cursed on the way up start looking good to me as an alternative to this path down.

We arrive at our place for the night. It comes close to my worst nightmare about places to sleep on a trek. The dark-wood, three-story building looks like something out of a documentary on areas that border the slums of India. The sole light bulb in our second-story room casts a near-useless amount of light. The sheets are damp, the quilts wetter—there wasn't enough sunshine to dry them today and electricity is too expensive to use dryers.

We put our boots on the balcony outside our room in case we missed removing any leeches. One clings to my arm. Reflexively, I pull it off and toss it over the railing and then worry it may have landed on someone. The spot where the leech was gorging itself continues to bleed. I apply pressure, but it keeps bleeding. Joel digs out a band aid from his pack. He stretches it tightly across the incision left at the feeding site. The bleeding slows.

Our next door neighbors, an Israeli couple, step out onto the balcony. We exchange hellos and head downstairs for dinner. They sit with the large group they are part of; we sit at a table for two and order cheese pizza, a welcome change to our diet. It's delicious and gives us the fuel we need to get ready for bed. The line for the European style bathroom is twelve deep. I opt to use the Nepali toilet—no line. Besides, I don't want to follow twelve people into a bathroom with no airing-out time between rounds.

We brush our teeth at a communal sink outside the bathrooms and then, exhausted, head to our room, place the sleeping bags we borrowed from the hotel in Pokhara on top of the wet bed and wrap ourselves in them. With headlamps secured to our foreheads, we start to read. The divide between our room and the next must be no more than a quarter-inch thick. If we spoke Hebrew we would understand everything the Israeli couple whispers to each other.

I read until my eyes close, thankful this night will be over soon.

Chapter Thirteen

# SALTED DOWN

## (Tadapani to Ghandruk)

*Sunday, September 11—Trek Day 4*

It's 8:30 a.m. when we leave Tadapani and head for
Ghandruk. The sun is shining and it feels good. Just before
we enter the rain forest, Gyanu motions for us to stop.
Reaching into his pocket, he extracts the pouch he
purchased in Pokhara the night before we began our trek,
and rubs some of its coarse white contents onto my hiking
boots.

"What's that?" I ask.

"Salt."

"What's it for?"

"Leeches. Keeps them away."

*What?* Why did Gyanu wait until now to take out
the salt? How much worse can the leeches be? I say
nothing; just let him finish what he's doing.

He rubs the remaining salt on Joel's boots and his.
It appears Urba, in flip-flops, doesn't need anything to fend
off leeches. Either he has a natural immunity or leeches
hate flip-flops.

The cool morning air makes Gyanu frisky; he cuts through the forest with a lightness and speed I'm convinced only a native Nepali can muster. Joel and I stay close behind, but lack the fluidity with which Gyanu moves. Two hours of power walking and we stop for a break at a teahouse set in a clearing. A young American couple comes up the path we're about to head down. We tell them about the rain forest ahead of them and leeches.

The woman distorts her mouth with loathing as the word "leeches" slides off her tongue.

Eager to share my new knowledge, I tell the couple, "We put salt on our hiking boots," and then confess, "It didn't stop the leeches completely; but it did help a little." I reexamine my thoughts and concede that perhaps there had been a battalion of leeches that the grains of salt defended me against.

They reach for the salt shaker on the table, empty it into their boots, and head on their way. I look for another shaker and reload; Gyanu's crystals washed away long ago in the wetness of the forest.

Joel distracts me from further salting down with a nudge and a nod toward the teahouse's patio where a man and woman sit hammering small rocks into course gravel. Joel fingers his camera, itching to take a shot. He catches Gyanu's eye and asks, "Is it all right?"

Gyanu, with a quick, subtle motion, shakes his head, no.

The desire to snap just one burns in Joel's eyes as he looks at the six-inch high pile of rocks encircling the Nepali couple and listens to the metallic clink of every patient strike.

We start down the trail; Joel takes one last longing look, and then follows along.

A few minutes later, Gyanu asks, "Did you take a picture?"

"No. You said not to."

Gyanu tells Joel that it would have been okay to take a picture. I stare in disbelief. Joel, usually good at hiding fury, looks as if he is about to spit fire, but doesn't say a word. Perhaps Gyanu's gesture just meant maybe. We're too far along to turn back.

We traverse flat and sloped areas, and slip down shallow steps made of carefully aligned, rectangular stones of uniform size, each bordered with gravel the couple at the teahouse may have made. The benign-looking beds of stone are as slick as tiles coated with thin ice. Joel falls twice; Gyanu is my failsafe walking stick. I welcome occasional dry stretches where I delight in the freedom to walk untethered.

In a relatively flat, open area where we pause for a break, Joel says, "See that?"

I follow his eyes and see he is looking at tall, rounded mountains that fold into each other; misty clouds float along their slopes. He points to a high ridge on the left and says, "That's where we've been. We climbed up and walked around that mountain."

"We did what? We were where?"

I can't believe what I'm hearing. My questioning eyes shift toward Gyanu who confirms what Joel said. I stand stunned; an urbanite at the core who grew up in Brooklyn among concrete and asphalt now stands in the middle of nature's paradise. A sense of awe and pride in accomplishment swells my mind and makes my heart beat extra strong. Gyanu, with a broad smile, allows me a moment to savor the feeling and then it is time to move on.

A look back at where we hiked.

We enjoy the absence of rain for two hours longer and then it begins to pour. As we re-enter the rain forest and head down stones and steps along a path smothered by ferns and unnamed leafy plants, Gyanu once again employs the minuet and handshake grips. I revert to sidesteps and jerks. Joel manages quite well on his own.

Up ahead, we see bright daylight that marks the edge of the rain forest. What we don't see is a fifty-foot waterfall that awaits us. We look down from its top and find that moss-covered stone steps along its left side descend into a broad shallow stream that runs past the waterfall's base. Two-feet wide at the top, the shallow steps fan out to four feet as they reach the bottom. I stare at them and calculate the chance I'll survive in one piece.

Sure-footed Urba, who is half-way down the wet mossy staircase, slips and falls, but manages to avoid cascading into the waterfall. This does not bode well for me still at the top re-doing my survival calculations; I increase the danger factor exponentially.

Gyanu calls to Urba who places our bags in a dry area on the other side of the stream and heads back up the steps.

"Urba will help you," Gyanu says to Joel.

"No. I don't need help."

"Yes you do," I am quick to say. After much prodding from Gyanu and threats from me, Joel gives in.

I grab Gyanu's extended hand as he turns to head down and nearly crush his bones with the fierceness of my grip. Knees trembling, feet slipping, eyes bulging, I reach the bottom unscathed. I make a mental note that wet moss could replace ice for skating rinks in the tropics.

I eye the partially submerged logs at the base of the waterfall that are the only means of crossing the stream. I just go; I'm done thinking.

I look back to see how Joel is faring. He's bounding along the logs having survived the waterfalls with no more than an occasional touch of his elbow by Urba. I'm reminded of how well-suited for this journey he is and the magnitude of the challenge it is for me.

By two-thirty, we skid to a halt outside a white, wood lodge that could pass for a Galveston Island beach resort. The brightness of its cerulean blue trim challenges the greyness of the afternoon.

"We are here," Gyanu says. I don't know how to interpret the foxy look on his face. It's been only six hours of hiking. It can't be we're done for the day.

"You're kidding!" I say, expecting yet another *not-this-one-the-one-up-there*.

"This is where we stay tonight," he says with unmistakable pride sparkling in his eyes.

The guesthouse, Hotel Manisha, is lovely by any standards and luxurious by a trekker's. A huge deck, with several wooden tables and chairs at which to relax or dine, has clotheslines strung along its edge ready to receive our wet clothes. Below it, there's another level with rooms and decking built into the mountainside. Faded Tibetan Buddhist prayer flags hang on lines strung diagonally between the two levels. Our bedroom, on the upper level, has its own bathroom, a hot shower, and, unlike the first place we stayed, it has towels.

We drop our things in the room and collapse onto wooden chairs by an outdoor table. I'm hungry enough to eat the menu in front of me. We order spring rolls, noodles, and soup—more than we usually eat for lunch and dinner combined.

While we wait for our food to arrive, I idly scan the deck until my eyes rest on a peddle-operated sewing machine like the one my mother had; a pillow to be mended lays on its work surface. The machine requires no electricity, just foot power to operate. I snap a picture and reminisce about how hard it was for me as a child to get my feet to rock back and forth on the broad pedal in the steady rhythm necessary to turn the wheel that plunges the sewing needle up and down.

Hotel Manisha. Pedal operated sewing machine.

The noodles and soup arrive with something that looks more like vegetarian calzones than spring rolls. We gobble everything down. It's all delicious.

Content, Joel showers and takes a nap. I shower, hang damp clothes out to dry, and then lean on the wooden railing at the edge of the deck taking in the lush greenery. From this perch, still high in the mountains, I gaze down at terraced rice paddies like the ones we gazed up at the beginning of the trek. One hundred steps or more lead to a lodge further up from our hotel. I watch three school girls dressed in dark blue skirts and sweaters climb the steps and then disappear from view as they move past the lodge at the top of the steps.

Distance and space silence all but the sound of bells that echo through the cool mountain air and signal the approach of a caravan of small pack horses. Shepherded by a young boy, his charges climb the same steps the girls climbed.

View from hotel patio. Pack horses climbing steps.

Our stay at this hotel more than makes up for last night. If the clouds clear, we will be able to see Annapurna South's peak in the morning. For now, I'm content to take in the beauty of the mountains we have climbed and walked around.

Chapter Fourteen

# THE LAST LEG

(Ghandruk to Nayapul)


*Monday, September 12—Trek Day 5*

This is it. The last day. Just a half-day's hike ahead of us. I put on the clean top I've been saving for the occasion. Joel looks as refreshed and ready to move on as I do. It's 8:15, forty-five minutes later than we had planned to leave hoping to arrive in Nayapul ahead of the afternoon rains. Clouds hide the Annapurna Mountain peaks, but I'm too happy to feel disappointment.

A light fog adds a quiet eeriness to the landscape as we head down the mist-shrouded mountain. An occasional stone house stands alongside the path. I bounce along, my face set in a smile; there are just 3,000 feet to descend on this quiet morning. The open vistas that stretch before us contrast sharply with the myopic views we experienced hiking through rain forests.

Not far along, a short, stocky Nepali man comes up the path and approaches us, eager to engage in conversation; his step is bouncier than mine and his smile broader. I can't tell if his exaggerated friendliness is normal or if he's a bit simple-minded; I haven't seen such exuberance from anyone along the trails.

He sets down a package he is carrying on a stone wall, bypasses Joel and Gyanu, and comes directly to me.

"Boyfriend?" he asks in his limited English.

"No. He's my husband."

"No. No husband. Boyfriend!" A chuckle follows.

I smile; he comes closer. With two hands he encircles the top of my right thigh and squeezes his way down to my ankle. I follow his hands in disbelief. Is this the way Nepali men get acquainted with Nepali women? He must be gauging whether or not I'd make a good wife who could handle the daily climbs up and down the mountain.

Embarrassed and confused over whether or not this man is normal, I give an uncomfortable smile and look toward Joel and Gyanu standing idly on the path. Neither comes to my rescue.

The man rises from my ankle and squeezes my right arm the same way he had my leg. I guess he can't believe the absence of muscle because he does it again and then goes back to my leg. He steps away and heads toward the cloth-wrapped object he had set on the wall. I breathe easier; he's done with me. My lack of upper body strength must have discouraged him from claiming me.

With nods, smiles, and fanfare, he unwraps what looks like a foot-and-a-half long, pale green watermelon. He cradles it in his arms, and rocks it like a baby.

"What is it?" I ask Gyanu.

"A cucumber. He grew it. It is like the one you ate last night. He is bringing it to the hotel."

I take a picture of the man, so proud of his "baby" and happy to pose." We say, "Namaste," and move on.

Nepali man bringing a cucumber he grew to the hotel.

By nine o'clock, parts of the path start to dry from last night's rain. Now I can look up at what's around me instead of down at my feet. By ten after nine, just as we approach a steep decline, it starts to rain. Gyanu takes my hand and prevents a dozen wipe-outs. Joel slips and slides behind me, but doesn't complain.

The rain continues on and off most of the morning. In between wettings, expansive views open revealing cultivated land with one and two-story homes tucked among terraced fields. Stripes of light-green soy plants meander through acres of bright green rice.

A four-foot high stone wall that curves along the path leads to a rough-hewn wooden gate left open. Beyond it lays a lush green field with tall, leafy trees and dense shrubs lining its periphery. An artist's hand could not make the scene more perfect.

Joel and I catch up to Gyanu and Urba as they sit near the edge of a canyon and gaze across the broad expanse. Strings of waterfalls, like tinsel tossed on a Christmas tree, stream down the opposite side and plunge into a river at the canyon's base.

"That is where we are going. Down to the river," Gyanu tells us. I nod but can't bring myself to look over the edge of the chasm. He rises, indicating it's time to move on.

One of several strings of waterfalls.

The land begins to slope more gently. The sun shines through and our rain jackets come off as we hike to our next stop, a teahouse. I look forward to recharging with canned pineapple juice—it has been my drink of choice along the trek.

Four Russians—a fiftyish mother, two thirtyish daughters, and their male friend are at the teahouse when we arrive.

"I saw you come into the dining room at Hotel Manisha last night. You didn't stay very long," I say wondering why they had sat at a table, looked at a menu, eyed each other, and left without a word.

"We were tired," volunteers one of the daughters in Russian accented English.

"I thought I was going to die," adds the other daughter, her eyes emphatically wide.

They glance at each other, laugh, and then the mother adds, "We hiked for fifteen hours."

"What?" A mixture of pain, admiration, and compassion accompany my exclamation.

"Yes, yesterday we hiked from Ghorepani to Ghandruk."

They're doing the five-day trek in four and did not stop for a night in Tadapani as we had. I wonder why. If they had done the trip in five days instead of four, they would have been only half as miserable as they were last night.

"Did you climb Poon Hill?" I ask.

"Yes!"

Eager to share the excitement of our experiences, I ask, "Did you see the peaks?"

"We got up at four, climbed to the top, and there were no peaks. It was too cloudy to see anything. We went back down."

"Oh," is all I can muster.

I know from Gyanu that the people who climbed Poon Hill the day before us—and now I learn that the ones who climbed a day after us—were not as lucky as Joel and I had been. I change the subject before the Russians have a chance to ask about our climb; I don't want to let them know what they missed.

"Did you come through the rainforest in the dark?" I ask, awed by their endurance.

"Yes."

"How could you see?"

"We had headlamps; but they did no good. Look, I'm all scratched," says a daughter. The Russian man laughs and shakes his head. He displays the scratches on his arms and shins.

"Were there leeches?"

"Yes. We were too tired to care."

I don't know how they can smile. Maybe they are giddy knowing this will be over soon. Their guide summons them and they move on. Gyanu tells us it's time for us to leave as well; this will be the last leg of the trip.


We continue to wind down the mountain. The dryness and more gradual descent allow us to walk quickly. I take the lead for the first time in almost five days. I turn right at a fork in the road only to hear Joel say, "Not that way!" He turns to Gyanu and says, "Louise is going back up the mountain!" I assure him I feel great, but not great enough to climb back up.

An hour later, we pause to catch our breaths alongside the path. From a ledge just above our heads, a toddler girl squats and watches us in silence. My camera is tucked inside Joel's backpack; he makes no move to let me get it. He must be tired of putting it in and taking it out each time the rain starts and stops. I don't dare insist; both he and Gyanu bear expressions that make it clear that all they want to do is get down the mountain. I'm just starting to enjoy myself.

The toddler's mother comes up a path hidden by a mound, takes her daughter by the hand, and walks her back into the house. Not a smile, not a word. It must be hard to maintain privacy with strangers hiking up and down, especially if you have an adorable child that trekkers like to coo over.

We pass a water buffalo lying in the shade under a lean-to; his enormous body fills the space end to end. As he gazes lazily out from the shelter, he reminds me of women leaning on windowsills of tenement houses watching the comings and goings of neighbors and strangers.

Water buffalo lounging in the shade.

I can't help but stare at the slender men who move up the mountainside with slow, measured strides carrying loads on their backs of furniture as large as armoires and irregularly shaped slabs of stone the length of their bodies—burdens too cumbersome for horses.

A man and woman walk in front of us carrying a baby in a woven basket hung on the woman's back. Watching from the comfort of her carrier, the baby studies us as she wobbles to the rhythm of her mother's steps.

A woman squats on the side of the road near a small stream and scrubs laundry on a smooth rock; her toddler daughter squats beside her scrubbing a small cloth of her own.

Further down, we see chickens perched on a railing gawking at a restaurant sign that advertises lunch without knowing they may be invited as well.

Checking out the lunch offerings.

Across from it stands a small billboard that says in Nepali, followed by English, *"Welcome to Dangsing Village Development Committee,"* and in capital letters, "OPEN DEFICATION FREE ZONE." Joel, whose work entails community development, can't resist snapping a picture to show back home. We laugh and take comfort in knowing that there were no indications of "open defecation" anywhere along the trails we hiked; Nepali toilets enclosed in sheds were available at every teahouse.

For the final two hours of the trek we walk along a pebbly road that parallels the glacier-fed river into which the waterfalls we passed empty. The turbulent waters are like ones seen on extreme sports programs multiplied by two. The river's grey murky color contrasts with the clear streams we've crossed.

I ask about the murkiness and Gyanu tells me, "When the glaciers melt, mud and stones come down, too." He tightens his lips, "There used to be snow even in March. Last couple of years, no more in March. Global warming." He shrugs his shoulders and moves on leaving me to ponder his words. He doesn't need lengthy scientific reports to document climate change; he looks up and sees it firsthand.

Gyanu marches ahead of us, stopping for nothing. He is in a hurry to get back to meet with clients that he has lined up to take on a trek tomorrow.

The hot sun replaces the humidity that made perspiration drip into my ears the past few days. I zigzag through patches of shade to escape the sharp rays even for an instant. Their intensity makes Joel and me not want to linger. We hustle to keep pace with Gyanu. There is no stopping for lunch; we share a snack bar we had in Joel's backpack for emergencies and give a second one to Gyanu.

At 3:30, almost seven hours after leaving the hotel, we arrive at Nayapul, where our trek began. As we pass the first checkpoint we had encountered five days ago, we see a group of eight grey-haired men and women with backpacks and walking sticks. In a booming voice, their guide tells them, "We have a seven-hour hike ahead of us. Let's get going."

Their eyes shift slowly from the guide to the path and their faces turn as grey as their hair.

We arrive at the snack shacks where we were dropped off and will be picked up. Strange to us at the beginning of our trek, they now feel as welcoming as a neighborhood candy store. Joel heads for a seat and a coke; I savor a can of juice. We salute each other. "WE DID IT!"

Joel and I in Nayapul at the end of the trek.

Chapter Fifteen

# ONE LAST PEEK

The driver hunches over the steering wheel, staring between wiper swipes that smear rain across the windshield. He honks the car horn furiously as he rounds blind curves and mutters things in Nepali I don't need to understand. We're headed to Pokhara on the same eroded road we traveled going to Nayapul five days and a lifetime ago. I relax next to Joel and Urba as we sit shoulder to shoulder in the rear seat, close my eyes to what lies ahead, and say to myself, "What is, *is*."

The sun comes out as we arrive at the Hotel Gurkha Haven, the same hotel we stayed at in Pokhara before the trek. This time we are given the penthouse room—a large, airy, rooftop suite with a sitting area, spacious sleeping area, large bathroom, and an air conditioner that works. I wash our boots at a spigot and drain tucked into a corner of the roof. There's no getting rid of their stench; they remain parked outside our door. I make a mental note to spray them with a disinfectant as soon as I can find some.

By the time we shower we're so tired that we can drag our bodies no further than the hotel dining room for dinner. I choose dal bhat—the yellow lentil soup mixed with rice that I have been living on for days. Mixed grilled vegetables and potatoes accompany the meal and make it extra delicious. Joel orders the same fare.

Gyanu, his hair still wet from his shower, stops by to chat before heading off to meet his next client. He turns to me and says, "If you come back in March and do the same trek, everything will be different."

"Why is that?" I ask.

"It is dry season."

Dry season? Hmmm. I can see Joel's eyes lighting up. He would like to do the twelve-day trek to Annapurna Base Camp. He has my blessings, and I hope friends to go with him.

Gyanu tells us that in spring, fields of corn will replace the rice fields. Philodendron trees will be covered with pink, red, and white blossoms changing the dark green forest into a giant bouquet. He leaves us to entertain visions of what it would be like if we trekked again.

That night, when I begin to fall asleep, my body jerks as if I'm falling into a void. I have had that feeling many times before, but this time there are more specifics— I'm slipping on rocks, and falling backwards.

Sun shines through a large window and nudges me awake early the next morning. In my peacefully groggy state, images float through my mind of thin, light-green blades of rice planted in fields edged with dense, dark-green rain forests. I see women in colorful clothing—reds, oranges, yellows—standing by teahouses, their metal sheet roofs weighted down with mini boulders. I marvel at men and women with overfilled baskets strapped to their backs gliding up and down the trails I struggled to conquer. Their gracefully borne burdens remind me of how important it is for the people who live on the mountain to have only those things that can be used and reused.

I pry one eyelid open and squint at the window through which the morning sun streams. What I see makes my other eye pop open. I give an unceremonious shove to my somnolent husband, swing my legs over the side of the bed, and yell, "Mountains!"

We throw clothes on, grab cameras, and run up the stairs to the upper level of the roof. There they are, the Annapurna peaks, glowing as they rise well above the clouds. We look at each other, smile knowingly, deeply satisfied, and then return our gaze to the mountains until clouds fade the view from our eyes, but not from our memories.

View of the Annapurna peaks from the
Hotel Gurkha Haven in Pokhara.

Am I glad I trekked?

Yes.

Would I do it again?

No.

Never? What about in March?

Ask me again in six months.

# EPILOGUE

Six months later Joel had a different mountain to climb. The adventurer in the family, the protector, lay in an Intensive Care Unit connected to tubes and monitors. The ski helmet he had worn saved his life when he tumbled downhill over the tips of his skis onto icy, packed snow. Seven weeks of his denying anything was seriously wrong ended when he came to me and said, "I need help."

I turned and saw bloodied arms and legs, the result of four spills while bike riding. I taped him with band aids and plastered him with four-inch gauze pads.

"I've made an appointment to see a doctor on Monday."

It wasn't for the scrapes and bruises; it was for the headaches, loss of balance, and increasing loss of control of his left hand—secrets he had kept from me.

"Would you like me to come with you?"

"Yes."

That's when I knew something was really wrong—he had never before asked me to accompany him to a doctor's office.

Monday couldn't come fast enough. After a brief neurological exam, the physician ordered us to go directly to an imaging center to have an MRI. When we arrived, we didn't spend any time counting minutes in a waiting room; they were ready for us.

Shortly after the MRI was completed, Joel returned to the reception area. A nurse at the front desk muttered words into a phone, but mostly listened. She passed the phone to Joel who turned pale. He said nothing, just handed the phone to me.

"Get him to the emergency room STAT! They're waiting for him."

This is not the place to tell the whole story of what followed Joel's accident. Our trek was an experience that deserves its own space, unclouded by anything else. But the two events that occurred within months of each other are, to me, fatefully related. I'll keep the telling short.

The subdural hematoma that Joel had ignored, or at least hid from the family including me, developed a life of its own. It formed a membrane and its own vascular system, and grew into a mass large enough to push Joel's brain off center. Two surgeries, seizures, five days in the ICU, six more days in the hospital, eight days at a rehabilitation center to learn how to walk again, two months of physical therapy, and Joel was just beginning the road to recovery.

Three months after the surgery, we traveled to our home in the mountains of New Mexico—ninety-five hundred feet high and miles away from contractual and volunteer work that exhausted Joel and impeded his recovery. A week after we arrived, on a drive into town to see a play, he pulled into a parking lot, stopped the car, and said, "Get me to the hospital; my left arm is going numb and I'm losing my speech."

Lying in a bed in the emergency room, he suffered a series of seizures. They began and ended the same way—his left arm became numb, the left side of his face sagged, his speech became difficult, mumbled, incoherent, and then impossible. As the seizures progressed, they came closer together and increased in duration. Fully conscious, Joel used nods to communicate until a heavy dose of hospital-administered medication stopped the seizures.

The setback perplexed his Texas neurosurgeon and his neurologist; Joel had done so well with recovery. They speculated that the seizures were brought on by the high altitude at which our New Mexico home is located.

Nine months from his surgery date, to the amazement and delight of his doctors, Joel was ninety percent recovered; his mental faculties were sharp and sense of balance had returned.

"Can I ski again?"

I gulped. Didn't he know what he has been through and could go through again? Didn't he know how narrowly he escaped death or severe, permanent brain damage?

His neurosurgeon answered Joel's question, "It all depends on how important it is to you. If you sustain another head injury, you won't be as lucky as you were this time."

"Is it okay to bike ride?"

"Again, it depends on how important it is to you. You might want to try a recumbent bike. It's lower to the ground."

My heart sank; Joel is as likely to ride a recumbent bike as a tricycle . . . it's not going to happen. And, if I have my way, he won't be on a bike either.

I looked at his face and saw that the doctor's message had gotten through.


It's March 2013, trekking season in Nepal, when the philodendron trees in the Himalayas are in bloom. I want to go there. I want to do another trek, a longer one. But now it would be too dangerous. Instead of fearing *I* would fall and further damage my wrists or ankles, we both would have to fear that Joel might fall or the altitude would trigger seizures. I shudder when I think of  trying to get down a mountain and to the kind of medical help he'd need as seizures fire away, each one worse than the last one.

When I look back, I don't think the confluence of events that led to a trek can be attributed to chance alone. I don't believe it was by happenstance that the woman donated a trip to Kathmandu instead of Buenos Aires as she had originally intended. That she offered two weeks instead of the usual one. That only one person bid against Joel and dropped out while the price was well within our budget and well below the price paid for other trips. That the Nepali orphanage owner/travel agent sat next to me on the airplane and mentioned Poon Hill. That "Poon Hill" was the only name easy enough for me to remember and inquire about. That the Poon Hill inquiry locked us onto a course that, step-by-step, led to the trek.

If the Himalayas hadn't come our way in fall 2011, by spring 2012, in all likelihood, the door would have closed on Joel's dream due to his accident and I would have missed an adventure of a lifetime.

Perhaps a year from now the ending to this memoir will need to be re-written. We may be at the Annapurna Base Camp, six days into a twelve-day trek, Joel happy as a lark and me complaining.

# ADDENDUM

It is five years later. My husband has fully recovered. We are starting to think about trekking in the Himalayas again. Perhaps after we take our next big trip—a safari in Africa planned for next year.

# Appendix A
## When to Trek According to Gyanu
### (With My Comments Added)

| | |
|---|---|
| *March, April, early May*<br>  Beautiful flowers and<br>  flowering trees | Fewer streams; waterfalls are<br>  not as dynamic as in<br>  monsoon season<br>Book flights, places to stay,<br>  and treks well in advance |
| *Mid May through*<br>*September*<br>  Hardly anyone treks<br>  Lush fields, raging<br>  rivers and waterfalls<br>  Rain, mud, and leeches | No problem getting flights,<br>  rooms<br>May have problems<br>  scheduling a trek due to<br>  weather. (We trekked<br>  toward the end of monsoon<br>  season; our guide hadn't<br>  had a client since May.)<br>No queuing up for toilets or<br>  showers<br>Few people on the trails, no<br>  heads in the way of photos |
| *October*<br>  Lush fields after the<br>  monsoon<br>  Clear skies—no rain<br>  Peak season<br>  Colder, but not by<br>  much | People going up and down the<br>  trails constantly<br>Competition for rooms, toilets,<br>  showers, food<br>Have to book everything well<br>  in advance |
| *November*<br>  Still good hiking<br>  Colder | Still a lot of people, but fewer<br>  than in October |
| *December through*<br>*February*<br>TOO COLD | |

# Appendix B

## What to Bring on the Trek

If you don't want to travel on airplanes lugging hiking gear, plan to spend a couple of days in Pokhara gearing up. Items are inexpensive and in many cases can be sold back at the end of the trek. We saw trekkers hiking without porters or guides, but I would recommend having at least a guide. They are great planners, invaluable when things go awry, and in the event of an accident, they're priceless.

Our List:

- Hiking boots well broken in (get these in advance of a trip)
- Walking stick (optional but handy)
- Sleeping bag in case sleeping conditions are bad (we borrowed ours from the hotel for a very reasonable fee)
- Backpack with space for a bladder of water and enough room for:
  o Rain jacket with a hood
  o Plastic backpack cover for rainy season
  o Cameras
  o Extra batteries for cameras
  o Imodium and Gas-X or the equivalent

- o Antibiotic/liquid band aid
- o Band aids including blister band aids
- o Sun screen
- o Extra eye glasses or contact lenses
- o Tissues
- o Roll of toilet paper (remove the cardboard core and flatten)
- o Emergency contact numbers
- o Journal and pen or other recording means
- o Handheld flashlight
- Also packed
  - o Hat or cap
  - o Sunglasses
  - o Head lamp for hiking in the dark
  - o Medications
  - o Toothpaste and brush
  - o Bar of soap
  - o Deodorant
  - o Microfiber towel
  - o 2 pairs of socks (more in monsoon season because it's hard getting anything to dry)
  - o 2 pairs of underwear—one to wash, one to wear (more in monsoon season)
  - o 2 sweat-wicking tops (more in monsoon season)
  - o 2 long-sleeved tops for evenings

- Jacket for evening (We had layers—long-sleeve top, vest, and fleece jacket—to use on the morning climb to Poon Hill. Some trekkers were wearing ski jackets.)
- Pair of jeans for the evening
- Pair of sneakers for evenings (lets the hiking boots air out)
- Scissors
- Book to read or other nighttime entertainment

There are things you may want to add to the list; but this should get you started. Enjoy the journey.

# ABOUT THE AUTHOR

LOUISE FERRARO DERETCHIN is a writer, painter, educator, and hiker. She grew up in a Brooklyn, New York but traded walking on sidewalks for hiking on trails in the Southern Rockies. Her essays have been published in literary journals. She holds a Ph.D. in educational psychology and is a former editor of an Association of Teacher Educators research journal. To learn more about the author and her artwork, go to LouiseDeretchinFineArt.com.

Made in the USA
San Bernardino, CA
21 February 2017